CHALLENGING LEVEL

The Hunger Games

A Teaching Guide

by Mary Elizabeth

Community Strand

Dedicated to Nan,
who introduced me to
The Hunger Games.

Copyright © 2014 Mary Elizabeth
All rights strictly reserved.

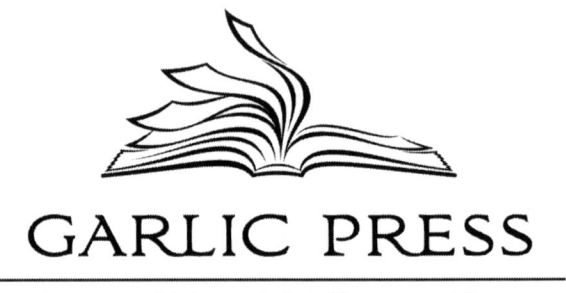

GARLIC PRESS
Educational Materials for Teachers and Parents

Remedia Publications Inc.
Scottsdale, AZ

www.remedia.com/garlic-press

In order to make it easy to use this teaching guide with digital and paperback versions, page numbers from *The Hunger Games* for use in locating vocabulary words, quotations, and chapter beginnings match both the Kindle eBook and the Scholastic, Inc. paperback ISBN -13: 978-0-545-42511-7

The purchaser of this book may reproduce any portion hereof, but not substantially the entire book, for classroom or nonprofit organizational use in an amount not to exceed one copy per pupil as an aid to classroom discussion. Copies may be made for not more than one course in the school or organization. Charging for copies or otherwise using the copies for commercial use is strictly prohibited.

Publisher: Remedia Publications Inc.
AUTHOR: Mary Elizabeth

ISBN 978-1-930820-00-5
Order Number GP-205

Table of Contents

Notes to the Teacher 5
   The Elements in this Literature Guide 5
   Teaching with Digital Editions 7
   Introducing the Literature 7
   Bibliography 9
   Suzanne Collins and *The Hunger Games* 9
   The Hunger Games Movies 9
   Common Core Correlation 10

               • Strategy 1: Beginning a Book 11

Part I "The Tributes"
Chapter 1   **The Reaping** 13
              • Strategy 2: Understanding the Reading Process 15
              • Strategy 3: Marking a Text 17
              • Strategy 4: Plot—Identifying the Overall Design of a Story 18
              • Strategy 5: Identifying the Narrator 19
Chapter 2   **The Volunteer; the Boy with the Bread** 20
              • Strategy 6: Interpreting Characterization 22
              • Strategy 7: Plot—Foreshadowing and Flashback 23
              • Strategy 8: Analyzing Choices 24
              • Writer's Forum 1: Writing a News Story 26
Chapter 3   **Goodbyes; the Trip to the Capitol Begins** 27
              • Strategy 9: Relating Setting and Mood 29
Chapter 4   **Tributes Confront Haymitch; Arrival at the Capitol** 30
              • Strategy 10: Forming Hypotheses 31
              • Writer's Forum 2: Comparing and Contrasting 32
Chapter 5   **The Stylists Create a Girl on Fire** 33
              • Strategy 11: Interpreting Names 35
Chapter 6   **The Avox** 36
              • Strategy 12: Understanding Symbolism and Motifs 37
Chapter 7   **Training; Impressing the Gamemakers** 38
Chapter 8   **The Scoring; How Katniss and Gale Met** 40
              • Strategy 13: Understanding Character Traits as Ranges 41
Chapter 9   **The Interviews** 42
              • Strategy 14: Identifying References, Allusions, and Parody 44
Test: Chapters 1–9 45

Part II "The Games"
Chapter 10   **"An Object of Love"; "To Die as Myself"** 46
Chapter 11   **The Games Begin; Search for Water; Peeta Joins Careers** 48
              • Strategy 15: Reading Dialogue 49
              • Writer's Forum: 3 Writing Dialogue 50
Chapter 12   **Finding Water; the Wall of Fire** 51
Chapter 13   **On Fire; Treed** 52
Chapter 14   **Tracker Jackers; the Silver Bow; Peeta Saves Katniss** 53
              • Strategy 16: Plot—Distinguishing Types of Conflic 54
Chapter 15   **An Ally and a Plan** 55
              • Writer's Forum 4: Writing First-Person Narration 56

Table of Contents, *cont.*

Chapter 16	**Blowing Up the Careers' Stash**	57
Chapter 17	**Katniss Loses Her Hearing; Rue in Trouble**	58
	• Strategy 17: Engaging with Text Through Imaging	59
	• Strategy 18: Understanding Cliffhangers	60
Chapter 18	**Rue's Death; Rule Change**	61
	• Strategy 19: Analyzing Lyrics	62
	• Writer's Forum 5: Writing Lyrics	64
Test: Chapters 10–18		65

Part III "The Victor"

Chapter 19	**Finding Wounded Peeta; the Cave**	66
	• Writer's Forum 6: Writing Description	67
Chapter 20	**Prim's Goat; Invitation to a Feast**	68
	• Writer's Forum 7: Composing an Anecdote	69
Chapter 21	**The Gamemaker's Feast; Death and Medicine**	70
Chapter 22	**Feelings on Display; Haymitch's Feast**	71
Chapter 23	**Thresh's Death; Foxface's Death**	72
	• Strategy 20: Revising Hypotheses	73
Chapter 24	**Last Night in the Cave; Driven to the Lake**	74
	• Writer's Forum 8: Writing a Possible Ending	75
Chapter 25	**Muttations; Second Rule Change; More Berries; Victors**	76
Chapter 26	**Recovery Period; Haymitch's Warning**	77
	• Strategy 21: Interpreting Irony	78
	• Strategy 22: Tracing the Hero's Journey	79
	• Strategy 23: Analyzing Diction and Style	80
Chapter 27	**Highlights; Exit Interview; Train Ride Home**	81
	• Strategy 24: Rereading a Book	83
	• Strategy 25: Identifying Themes	84
	• Writer's Forum 9: Composing a Book Review	85
	• Writer's Forum 10: Comparing Two Treatments	86
Test: Chapters 19–27		87

Theme Pages
- Taste — 88
- Identity — 88
- Integrity — 88
- Courage — 89
- Friendship and Loyalty — 89
- Leadership and Government — 89
- Good and Evil — 89

Answer Pages — 90
   Chapter, Strategy, Writer's Forum, and Test Page Answers in Order — 90
   Theme Page Answers — 112

Notes to the Teacher

The Discovering Literature Series is designed to develop students' appreciation for good literature and to improve reading comprehension. The Challenging Level focuses on reading strategies that help students construct meaning as they read, as well as make connections between and among texts. The strategies taught in each guide reflect the demands of the particular literature selection, and material can be adapted or skipped to suit both class focus and students' developmental level, or even adapted for book club use.

Every teacher of literature faces a quandary in that the experience of literature—suspending one's disbelief and getting lost in the world of a story (aesthetic reading)—and the analysis of literature (efferent reading) are mutually exclusive: it is impossible to engage in both simultaneously. Thus, this guide is designed to be used with at least three different reading modes:

- **Aesthetic/Analytic** Students read the book through first for the experience of the story (with or without vocabulary preparation, depending on the student) and use the guide afterwards to work on comprehension and analysis;
- **Chapter-by-Chapter** Students read after limited preparation (possibly only vocabulary), but a thorough check-in on comprehension and analytic understanding after each chapter ensures comprehension;
- **Guided Reading** Students' reading is scaffolded by, for example, using one or more of the Journal and Discussion Topics to provide a purpose for reading each chapter (being careful to select questions that do not give away major plot elements), and following up as in the other modes.

For *The Hunger Games*, any reading is likely to be influenced by the movie version if students have seen it, limiting students' ability to imagine the story with the sole influence of Collin's words. If your students are in this situation, it is best to address the influence explicitl , comparing and contrasting the versions..

THE ELEMENTS IN THIS LITERATURE GUIDE

Page Numbers

To make it easier to teach students who have different editions, page numbers that match both paperback and Kindle editions are used to locate vocabulary words, quotations, and chapter beginnings.

Chapter Pages

The **Chapter Vocabulary** identifies challenging words and provides page numbers and definitions for the specific usage in the book. Introducing the **Chapter Vocabulary** prior to students' reading in any mode can help insure that their reading is not disrupted by unknown words, but since there may be a large amount of unfamiliar vocabulary, you may wish to do this over a period of time, not all at once.

More interesting vocabulary activities will be possible if you treat multiple chapters' worth of vocabulary at once, and more meaningful vocabulary exercises will improve retention. A Vocabulary Study feature including suggested activities and vocabulary for the entire trilogy is offered at the end of *Mockingjay: A Teaching Guide*. If you do choose to work by chapter, you could have students:

1. identify relationships between and among words, creating a web or other graphic that shows these relationships and adding related words.
2. keep an eye out for multiple meaning words and synonyms (words that Collins uses in multiple, different meanings are marked "MM" in the vocabulary lists.)

Notes to the Teacher

3. use a set of words in a piece of writing, for example a poem, a personal anecdote, a one-act play, or a journal written in the persona of a character;
4. research the etymology of a set of vocabulary words;
5. make and exchange puzzles made with vocabulary words;
6. write and exchange cloze exercises using the vocabulary words;
7. identify subcategories of vocabulary, for example, words about nature and hunting, verbs, words naming character attributes, six-syllable words, etc.

The **Journal and Discussion Topics** can be used as prompts for entries in students' Reading Response Journals if you choose to use them, as questions for discussion to help students become deeply engaged with the literature, and/or to check comprehension. If you wish to interact with students using their journals, the dialogue will be facilitated if you periodically collect the journals and respond to students' comments. It is important for students to know beforehand whether their journals are private or public. Even if they are public, many educators believe that journals should not be corrected or graded, but only recorded as being used. You may also wish to keep your own journal.

Discussion can take place between partners, in small groups, or as a whole class. Students may also wish to reflect on the discussion in their journals. Discussion starters include:

1. review of predictions made for the chapter and whether they were accurate.
2. group retelling of the chapter in which everyone participates.
3. each group member sharing:
    a. the most striking moment in the chapter for him or her;
    b. a question she or he would like to ask the author or a character; or
    c. what he or she liked most or least about the chapter.
4. analysis of how the chapter relates to the preceding chapters.

The **Chapter Summary** for each chapter is included for teacher use only. While the name I've given to the chapter (Collins does not name her chapters) provides an at-a-glance review of the chapter, the summary has enough details to refresh your memory about specific contents of each chapter. The summaries should never be used to replace reading the work of literature. Note that while the suggested questions always include a summarization idea, these questions are couched so that the summaries provided in this book will not provide adequate answers.

Strategy Pages

Strategy Pages are developed to increase students' understanding of strategies they can use to enhance their understanding of literature. A strategic approach does not eschew teaching skills, but takes instruction farther by helping students understand how and when to deploy their skills, that is, choose appropriate skills to employ in various literary situations. Having a strategic understanding of how meaning is made by the interaction of authors' words and readers' understanding and imagination can lead to enriched reading experiences. Students will have the opportunity to consider topics such as:

- monitoring their reading process and comprehension
- marking the text in fruitful ways
- actively seeking out, identifying, and interpreting the elements of literature, such as plot, character, setting, mood, narration, theme, etc.

You may copy and distribute Strategy Pages. Students can answer on the back of the page or on a separate sheet of paper. Some Strategy Page questions require ongoing attention as the students continue reading.

Tests

At the end of each of the three parts of the novel, a comprehensive **Test** has been provided for your use. Each test includes vocabulary exercises and short essay topics. You may copy and distribute these pages, which students may complete with or without access to the text, as you decide.

6   *The Hunger Games: A Teaching Guide*

Writer's Forum Pages

Each **Writer's Forum** page presents instruction about a particular genre and directions for a particular writing task in that genre. Assignments draw on both the literature and students' own experience of the text. You can choose from these suggestions or substitute your own creative-writing ideas.

As you plan writing lessons, allow enough time for students to engage in the writing process:

- **Prewrite** (brainstorm and plan their work)
- **Draft** (give a shape to their ideas on paper)
- **Review** (revisit their work with an eye to improving it, on their own as well as with peers, with you, or with other reviewers)
- **Revise** (make changes that they feel will improve their draft)
- **Proofread** (check for accuracy in grammar, mechanics, and spelling)
- **Publish** (present their work to others in some way)

Theme Pages

There are several different ways to approach theme, starting with Strategy Page: Identifying Themes (p. 84) and the Theme Pages (pp. 88–89). You can also set this work in the context of other works of literature that focus on community using our other literature guides in "The Community" series or other works with a community theme, for example, these dystopias:

- *Animal Farm* or *Nineteen Eighty-Four* by George Orwell
- *Brave New World* by Aldous Huxley
- *Ender's Game* by Orson Scott Card
- *Fahrenheit 451* by Ray Bradbury
- "Harrison Bergeron" by Kurt Vonnegut
- "The Lottery" by Shirley Jackson
- *The Time Machine* by H. G. Wells
- *V for Vendetta* by Alan Moore and David Lloyd

A group of books with a similar theme can also throw light on Big Ideas. Big Ideas worth considering include the following:

- What makes a community?
- What does the community owe the individual and vice versa?
- How can individuals best respond when a community is or becomes unjust or otherwise damaging to individuals' interests?

Answer Pages

Possible responses are given in the **Answer Pages**. The responses include critical analysis of the novel that you may find useful. Students' answers are expected to be more developed than the sample answers in many cases.

TEACHING WITH DIGITAL EDITIONS

One of the advantages of many digital editions is the ready access to definitions of every word, but there are three reasons that it is not wise to rely on this in place of teaching vocabulary: 1) it interrupts the reader's experience of the story; 2) the definition offered may not match the use in the text; 3) the word may not appear (for example, Collins's neologisms). On the other hand, digital editions may allow adjustment of brightness, font, text size, and line length, giving the reader more control over the reading experience, and may also allow note-taking. An eReader may be able to read the book aloud, but you may wish to check the quality of this feature.

INTRODUCING THE LITERATURE

How you choose to introduce the literature will likely depend on the student and reading mode. For Aesthetic/Analytic reading, you may simply hand the student an edition and allow the author to unfold the world of the story in his or her own way. To prepare students to read the work aesthetically, explain that in a work of fiction an author creates an imaginary world. An important task in beginning a literature selection is coming to terms with that world.

Notes to the Teacher

The Hunger Games: A Teaching Guide 7

Notes to the Teacher

When students need guidance and when you are teaching analysis, you can use this guide to help students contextualize *The Hunger Games* using Strategy 1: Beginning a Book, p. 11). After you have found out what, if any, familiarity students have with the book and author and what they have discerned about the genre and subject from glancing at their editions, you can provide any necessary background knowledge and, if it seems appropriate, correct any misapprehensions students have, e.g., conclusions drawn from the movie don't fit the book. You may wish to specifically encourage students to—as much as they can—set aside what they know from outside sources and read the text on its own terms.

Whatever mode students are using, it is a good idea to point out that it is possible to consciously assess one's own understanding and that this process is called *metacognitive reflection*. Also point out that doing so may interrupt the experience of the story until such reflection becomes seamlessly integrated into the reader's process. If this is your first discussion of metacognitive reflection with your students, you may wish to model the process using a think-aloud approach as you go through the questions for the title and first few paragraphs in Strategy 1 (for aesthetic reading, skip over the others for now). Simply read aloud the portion of *The Hunger Games* (or another book, if you don't want to influence students' reading) needed to answer the questions, and speak aloud your thoughts as you formulate your responses, making explicit the connections and prior knowledge you are developing in your thoughts. Continue with whichever prereading activities you have determined are appropriate.

Sample Lesson Plan

It's likely that students will eventually end up reading chapter-by-chapter. If they are using the aesthetic/analytic approach, this will be their second reading of the book. At this point, all students can engage in prereading, during reading, and after reading activities geared for their abilities and needs.

Prereading Activities: Choose these activities based on how much prereading guidance students need and what can be handled after they read. Prereading activities may include:

- previewing vocabulary and doing a vocabulary exercise;
- reviewing the developments of the previous chapter(s); and
- reviewing predictions.

During Reading: Students can read with their Reading Journals handy, if it suits their reading mode: if they are experiencing the story and don't want to be interrupted to do a journal entry, allow them to write in the journal after they read. If students need guidance as they read, you may wish to give them some of the journal and discussion topics before they read to help focus their attention. Additional journal activities they can use with every chapter include the following:

- recording questions they have about what they have read;
- recording associations they have made between this text and other texts, experiences, or situations; and
- taking notes on the images and/or feelings the text evoked.

After Reading: Students can complete the Journal and Discussion Topics, and the Writer's Forum and Strategy Pages and Test (if any). You may wish to end each discussion by having students explain and note their predictions.

Adding a Social Dimension

If you'd like to add a social dimension to your literature classes, I recommend the Subtext app for iPad, which will allow you to purchase *The Hunger Games* from Google Books from within the app and have a private reading experience with your class, while providing a forum for tracking literary elements, making predictions, noting emotions, taking polls, etc. Since students will have access to others' comments, you may want to have them read chapters on their own first to avoid interrupting their initial reading experience. For more information, go to http://subtext.com.

BIBLIOGRAPHY

As you and your students immerse yourselves in this work of literature, you may wish to consult other works. Here is a brief list of works that may be useful:

Blasingame, James and Collins, Suzanne. "An Interview with Suzanne Collins." Journal of Adolescent & Adult Literacy, Vol. 52, No. 8 (May, 2009), pp. 726-727.
Collins, Suzanne. *Catching Fire*; *Mockingjay* (Scholastic: New York, 2009; 2010).
Collins, Suzanne. *Underland Chronicles* (Scholastic: New York, 2003–7).
Dunn, George A. and Michaud, Nicolas, eds. *The Hunger Games and Philosophy*: A Critique of Pure Treason. (John Wiley & Sons: New Jersey, 2012).
Pharr, Mary F. and Leisa A. Clark, eds. *Of Bread, Blood, and* The Hunger Games. (McFarland & Company, Inc., Publishers: Jefferson, NC, 2012

SUZANNE COLLINS AND THE HUNGER GAMES

Collins was born in Connecticut in 1962, but the fact that her father was in the military meant that her childhood was spent at a number of locations in the U.S. and overseas. A military historian, her father shared his understandings of the world with his children, so Collins grew up with an awareness of war. After spending a number of years writing for children's television shows, she met James Proimos, an author of children's books, who inspired her and to whom *The Hunger Games* is dedicated. Her fantasy series *The Underland Chronicles* was published between 2003 and 2007 and treats war in a variety of ways. *The Hunger Games* trilogy, the first novel of which was published in 2008, progresses from a war game in the first book, to a revolution in the second, and a war in the third.

The story of *The Hunger Games* sprang from several roots. On the one hand, Collins—a fan of Greek mythology—was influenced by the story of King Minos of Crete imposing a yearly tribute of seven youths and seven maidens on Athens, and thrusting them into the Labyrinth, where they were slain by the Minotaur. Theseus, son of the king of Athens goes as one of the seven youths, slays the Minotaur, and ends the practice. On the other hand, an incident of channel surfing during which she was going back and forth between a reality TV program and real war coverage and the two began to blend in her mind was another source of inspiration.

THE HUNGER GAMES MOVIES

Collins wrote the initial screenplay for the movie version, which came out in 2012.

The differences between the book and the movie are likely to come up as you teach the novel. Collins herself pointed to three important differences in an interview with Scholastic:

> **Q: We understand you worked on the initial screenplay for a film to be based on *The Hunger Games*. What is the biggest difference between writing a novel and writing a screenplay?**
>
> A: There were several significant differences. Time, for starters. When you're adapting a novel into a two-hour movie you can't take everything with you. The story has to be condensed to fit the new form. Then there's the question of how best to take a book told in the first person and present tense and transform it into a satisfying dramatic experience. In the novel, you never leave Katniss for a second and are privy to all of her thoughts so you need a way to dramatize her inner world and to make it possible for other characters to exist outside of her company. Finally, there's the challenge of how to present the violence while still maintaining a PG-13 rating so that your core audience can view it. A lot of things are acceptable on a page that wouldn't be on a screen. But how certain moments are depicted will ultimately be in the director's hands.
>
> (http://www.scholastic.com/thehungergames/media/suzanne_collins_q_and_q.pdf)

So, students who have seen the movie and try to avoid reading the book are likely to make mistakes in point of view, leaving out details, and providing different descriptions of the violence.

Notes to the Teacher

The Hunger Games: A Teaching Guide

Common Core

The Common Core State Standards Initiative proposes educational standards that aim to "provide a consistent, clear understanding of what students are expected to learn, so teachers and parents know what they need to do to help them." As of October 2013, 45 states and four US territories have adopted the Common Core Standards. The following chart shows how exercises and activities in this teaching guide align with the relevant Common Core standards. Because this guide may be used across a range of ages and grade levels, the chart refers to the key content of each standard across grades 6–12.

The Common Core Standards emphasize skills and knowledge, so you may wonder why this teaching guide emphasizes *strategies* and how strategies and skills are related. A *strategy* is the knowledge of when and how to deploy your skills for the most effective results. If you have skills and don't know when and how to use them, they don't do much good. The strategy lessons in this teaching guide provide instruction in skills, contextualized with information about when and how to use them effectively.

STANDARD	PAGE NUMBER
Reading Standards for Literature	
1. Cite textual evidence	13, 20, 22, 31, 38, 54, 56, 68, 73, 74, 84, 85
2. Determine themes	12, 75, 84, 85, 86, 88–89
3. Analyze story development	plot development, 18, 23, 29, 31, 54, 73, 75, 79; characterization, 22, 41; character motivation and choices, 24
4. Determine meanings of words	meaning of words, 15–6; references and allusions, 17, 44, 46, 52; tone, 19, 22; figurative language, 59; rhyme, 62–3; onomatopoeia, 64; irony, 78; diction and style, 80
5. Analyze structure	cliffhangers, 60; conflict, 54; flashbacks, 23, 29; foreshadowing, 23, 75; lyrics, 62–3; overall plot, 18
6. Analyze point of view/narration	14, 19, 20, 27, 33, 36, 47, 48, 49, 51, 53, 55, 56, 70, 74, 78
7. Compare multiple versions	86
9. Compare/contrast texts	identify references, allusions, and parody, 44; *HG* with a reality television show, 65; *HG* with another "Community" book or dystopia, 84; the ending of *HG* with the ending of *The Giver* or *The Lord of the Flies*, 87; compare with brief quotations, 88–9
Writing Standards	
1. Write arguments to support claims	13, 19, 20, 31, 38, 42, 54, 73, 79, 85, 86
2. Write informative/explanatory texts	13–4, 20, 26, 27, 30, 33, 36, 38, 40, 42, 45, 46, 48, 51, 52, 53, 55, 57, 58, 61, 65, 66, 68, 70, 71, 72, 74, 76, 77, 81, 87
3. Write narratives	news story, 26; first-person narration, 56; anecdote, 69; possible ending 75
9. Draw evidence from literary texts	35, 44, 46, 52, 80, 86
10. Write a range of texts for various purposes/audiences	news story, 26; hypothesis, 31; comparison and contrast, 32; dialogue, 50; 1st-person narration, 56; anthem lyrics, 64; description, 67; anecdote, 69; possible ending, 75; book review, 85; comparison of two treatments, 86
Language Standards	
5. Understand figurative language, word relationships, and nuances	14, 35, 37, 45, 46, 52, 59, 87

Strategy 1   Beginning a Book

Directions: First, read the information. Then, answer the question or questions.

When an artist or craftworker sets about creating a work, there are a set of standard tools, techniques, and products available. The costume designer, for example, has many kinds of fabric, trim, and accessories available. The product may be an outfit for a man, woman, or child from any age or era, garb to make the wearer appear to be an animal, or a fantasy costume based on the designer's imagination. The techniques used may include various kinds of stitches, types of sleeve, neckline shapes, etc. In addition, there are certain conventions, such as standard color combinations, that the costume designer may choose to employ or not. The costume designer does not use every technique and material in every costume, and his or her choices are guided by the goal, which might be the answer to a question such as, "How can I effectively communicate my vision?" The viewer observing the finished product cannot see it all at one time. Moving closer and farther away, walking around the model, attending to details, silhouettes, colors, textures, and the effect of the whole, the viewer can come to understand the costume.

The novelist is an artist who works in words that create images, thoughts, and feelings in the reader. Like the costume designer, the writer may not be present when the audience experiences the product (in this case a book), but reading is, nevertheless, an act of communication in which both writer and reader play a part. The reader's understanding of the standard tools, techniques, and conventions of the writer help the reader to understand the writer's vision. This doesn't mean that every reader has the same experience: each reader brings an individual and unique understanding to the act of reading, so different readers will have different insights and feelings. As a result, discussion between and among readers can enrich the experience of all.

Beginning a book is particularly important because readers starting a book are entering new, uncharted territory. This is true even though they may have *prior knowledge* about the author, genre, and story through having read other books by the author, having read other books in the genre, or having seen a movie or heard an audio recording of the work they are about to read. When you are starting a work of fiction paying particular attention to the available clues can help you to enter the world of the story.

Title: It is a convention for a novel to have a title, found on the front cover, the spine, and the title page of a print edition and in the library and on the title page of an eBook. The title of the book may explicitly tell what the book is about, may hint about the story, or may seem very mysterious. Sometimes a book has a subtitle—a second part of the title written below the main title. Often, the subtitle appears only on the title page. The author's name appears on the title page as well.

Cover Illustration: Many books have a picture on the cover. The writer may or may not have had a voice in what appears, so the illustration may or may not represent the writer's vision; nevertheless, it can give you some idea of characters, setting, and plot in the story.

Copyright Page: The copyright page tells the dates of the book's publication. It can help you know whether the book is recent or older and whether it is an original version or edited, adapted, or translated.

Other Books By: Other books by the same author may be listed.

The Hunger Games: A Teaching Guide   11

Strategy 1, cont

Table of Contents: *The Hunger Games,* has named parts, but untitled chapters. Like the book title, book parts with names may reveal more or less about what happens in the book. It's worth looking at the eBook navigation guide to see this if you are reading a digital edition and there is no internal table of contents.

Inside Illustrations: Some books are illustrated throughout with drawings, paintings, photographs, etc. *The Hunger Games* does not have internal illustrations.

Back Cover Blurb: The note on the back cover of print editions is advertising, meant to give away enough of the story to pique your interest and convince you to buy the book. It doesn't necessarily reflect the writer's vision or the most meaningful view of the story. In addition, it may contain spoilers, so it is best avoided.

First Few Paragraphs: The first few paragraphs of the story provide the writer with the first opportunity to introduce the characters, plot, setting, and theme of the story. Read carefully to learn as much as you can about the world of the book.

1. Does the approach to beginning a book described here differ from what you usually do? If so, how?
2. What is your reaction to the title of the book?
3. Describe the cover illustration on your edition. What can you gather from it?
4. How long has it been since this book was first published?
5. What, if anything, do you already know about Collins, her works, or *The Hunger Games*?
6. What can you tell about the story from the part titles? How do they seem to relate to the book title? Which part might the cover illustration come from?
7. Read to "almost always enter the woods here" (p. 5). Describe the writing.
8. What is the narrator like? Can you trust the narrator's perceptions? How do you know? To whom is the narrator telling the story?
9. Who seem(s) to be the most important character(s)? How can you tell?
10. Where does the story take place? Is it a real setting or a setting created by the author? What special characteristics does the setting have?
11. What more do you hope to learn about the setting and the characters?
12. What clues are there to the genre of this story?
13. What does the theme or focus of the story seem to be?
14. What do you predict will happen next in the story?

Chapter 1

PART I "THE TRIBUTES"
The Reaping

Vocabulary

reaping 3 harvesting
vermin 3 worms
cocooned 3 wrapped up snuggly
entrails 4 internal parts of an animal
supple 4 flexibl
forage 4 provisions gathered from nature
sleep in 4 sleep until later than usual
deterrent 4 barrier to prevent action
predators 4 meat-eating animals; anything that preys on animals
sheath 5 case that is open at one end
venomous 5 poisonous
rabid 5 infected w/ rabies
poaching 5 trespassing to take game, fis
venture 5 start task w/ uncertain outcome
rarity 5 something extremely unusual
inciting 5 stirring to action
rebellion 5 armed resistance against one's government
turn a blind eye to 5 choose to ignore
mutter 6 say indistinctly and in low tones
blurt 6 say w/out considering results
indifferent 6 uncaring; unresponsive
food shortages 6 times of not enough food
thicket 6 dense bushes or shrubs
game 7 animals converted to food sources by hunting
pelt 7 an animal's hide or skin
puncture 7 hole made by piercing
mimics 7 imitates
maniacally 7 w/ unsuitable enthusiasm
tartness 7 sourness
verve 8 enthusiasm
apothecary 8 workplace for a dispenser of healing herbs
medicinal 8 healing; able to heal
brewed 8 soaked in hot water
remedies 8 medicines to cure ills
nook 9 a small recess or opening
teeming 9 fille
iridescent 9 shining like a rainbow
seeping 9 melting
preposterous 9 unreasonable; absurd
lard 9 fat from hogs, used for cooking
haggling 10 driving hard bargains
prey 11 animal hunted and killed for food
abounds 11 is plentiful
tad 11 small amount

take out 11 kill
being ironic 12 meaning the opposite of what is literally said
meager 13 inadequate, skimpy
rant 14 give a long, loud, angry speech
smoldering 14 feeling unexpressed anger
spoils 14 rewards of illegal activity
mandatory 16 required
perched 16 sitting in an elevated position, like a bird on a perch
perimeter 16 path around the edge
racketeers 17 those engaged in organized, illegal activities
claustrophobic 17 anxiety-causing due to lack of space
refuse 17 say no to
adjacent 17 bordering on; nearby
terse 17 brief
podium 17 platform for a speaker
escort 17 person who protects or guides
encroaching 18 advancing beyond usual limits
brutal 18 savage; inhuman
sustenance 18 food
prosperity 18 well-being
uprising 18 act of revolt or rebellion
obliterated 18 reduced to nothing
treaty 18 document that states terms of a war ending
treason 18 betraying one's government
tributes 18 payments that acknowledge another's power and control
wasteland 18 land where nothing grows
at the mercy of 18 under the control of
sacrifice 19 kill; murder
humiliating 19; embarrasing; causing shame
torturous 19 causing suffering
festivity 19 celebration
delicacies 19 choice, rare food
repentance 19 sorrow for one's wrongs
intones 19 speak in solemn monotone
unintelligible 19 not able to be understood
token 19 minimal
fend off 19 MM avoid; ward off
laughingstock 19 object of scorn
molest 20 bother
nauseous 20 sick to one's stomach

Journal and Discussion Topics

1. Now that you've read the first hapter, what do you think the story will be about? What evidence supports your conclusions?
2. *Reaping* has a special meaning in Panem (/pah NEHM/). What is it?
3. Is the reference to Prim's "warmth" literal, figurativ , or both. What makes you think as you do?
4. What incentive is there for Panem citizens to have children?
5. Why does the Capitol reap children rather than adults? Why age 12–18?

The Hunger Games: A Teaching Guide 13

Chapter 1, cont.

6. Who is exempt from the reaping?
7. How is citizenship in Panem different from citizenship where you live?
8. In what different ways does Katniss convey her feelings about the Capitol?
9. What does the geography of District 12 and the description of Panem's history suggest about the overall geography of Panem?
10. What is the effect of Katniss comparing the camera crews to buzzards?
11. Here is the definition of *treason* from the United States Constitution, Section 3:

    "Treason against the United States, shall consist only in levying war against them, or in adhering to their enemies, giving them aid and comfort. No person shall be convicted of treason unless on the testimony of two witnesses to the same overt act, or on confession in open court.

    The Congress shall have power to declare the punishment of treason, but no attainder of treason shall work corruption of blood, or forfeiture except during the life of the person attainted."

    (http://www.law.cornell.edu/constitution/articleiii)

    The latter part of the second paragraph refers to the limitations on inheritance from a person found guilty of treason. Given what we know of the Treaty of Treason, the definition of treason in anem differs in one important way from the definition in the first paragraph abo . Explain this key difference.

12. Summarize the chapter from Prim's point of view. Be sure to tell only what she knows, or could reasonably be expected to know.

Summary

Sixteen-year-old Katniss Everdeen, the first-person narrator, awakens in her home in the coal-mining Seam section of District 12 in the country of Panem to find that her younger sister—Prim (short for Primrose), aged 12—has left their shared bed to find comfort with their mother. She concludes that this is because today is "the reaping." Katniss gets dressed and illegally crosses the barb-wire-topped chain-link fence that surrounds the District to meet her hunting/poaching partner, Gale, a young man of 18.

Katniss's father had died in a mining accident when Katniss was 11, and their mother became withdrawn and "unreachable," leading Katniss to become the family provider using the hunting and gathering skills her father had taught her. Gale, whose father died in the same accident, does the same for his family. Outside the boundaries, Katniss and Gale allow themselves to express their negative feelings about the Capitol from which Panem is ruled and Capitol residents, particularly Effie Trinket, District 12's escort to the Hunger Games. They fish and gather, trading some of their take at the local black market, the Hob, before going to sell strawberries to the well-to-do mayor. The mayor's daughter, Katniss's classmate Madge, answers the back door. Irritated by her valuable gold pin, Gale can't hide his resentment of Madge's limited likelihood of being selected in the reaping. Katniss and Gale have chosen to have their names entered multiple times in addition to their regular, yearly entries in exchange for oil and grain to help their families survive, with the result that while Madge has only five entries, Katniss has 20, and Gale has 42. (It is Prim's first reaping, and she has only one.) Gale and Katniss each go home with their division of the spoils that were not sold. Katniss bathes and puts on one of her mother's lovely dresses from when she lived in town and worked at her parents' apothecary shop before she married a coal miner, and her mother puts Katniss's hair in an elaborate braid.

The entire population of District 12, about 8,000, squeezes into the town square or lines adjacent streets, with TV crews in place to cover the reaping for later broadcast to the entire country. The mayor, Effie Trinket, and an empty chair are on a stage. The mayor reads the history of Panem, founded on the ruins of North America after natural catastrophes and a brutal war. An uprising of the districts against the Capitol—which ended in the defeat of 12 districts and the annihilation of the 13th—ended with the Treaty of Treason, which established the Hunger Games, a televised arena spectacle that is required watching for all citizens and in which one girl and one boy tribute drawn by lot from each district in the "reaping" participates in a fight to the death. The last tribute remaining alive is named "victor" and gains a year of gifts for his or her district and a life of luxury for him- or herself. As names of the past winners of District 12 are read—there have only been two in 73 years—the only surviving winner, Haymitch Abernathy—the intended occupant of the empty chair—drunkenly stumbles onto the stage. Effie Trinket comes forward to choose the tributes, and from the jar with girls' names selects the single slip of paper imprinted with the name *Primrose Everdeen*.

Strategy 2

Understanding the Reading Process

Directions:
First, read the information. Then, answer the question or questions.

You've probably heard of *prewriting*—the term used to designate the planning you do as you prepare to write a text—but there's no comparable term *pre-reading*, even though when we read we have to:

- recognize black marks on the paper as letters and words;
- process the words in groups to construct meaning and figure out how phrases, clauses, and ideas are connected;
- relate the perceived meaning to what we already know about texts in general, texts of the same genre as the one we're reading, earlier information from this particular text, etc.;
- create in our minds the world of the text;
- apply our prior knowledge of facts, experiences, other texts, ideas, feelings, sensory data, and the like to help us understand what we have read;
- try to recollect the new sequence of events that make up the plot; and
- fill gaps left by the text (no text tells absolutely everything that happened) with our own elaborations.

With so much processing going on the first time we read a book—as we discover everything about a story for the first time, we may miss some aspects. It may help you to understand this if you think about the difference between a painting—which can be seen in its entirety in an instant—and a work of fiction—which not only takes all the steps mentioned above, but also unfolds in the reader's imagination over the time that it takes him or her to read it.

One approach that can help you deal with the complexity of a first reading is to keep an eye on your reading rate and adjust it as necessary. How quickly or slowly we read may be an aspect of reading we don't think too much about: it may be automatic for us to adjust our speed to cope with different kinds of texts and reading for different purposes. But let's just stop for a moment here and identify some of the purposes and text characteristics that might lead us to intentionally slow down our reading, and if necessary, reread material or use other approaches. (For information on marking a text, see Strategy 3: Marking a Text, p. 17; for more about rereading, see Strategy 24: Rereading a Book, p. 83.)

Reading Purposes	*How to Adjust*
Want/need to remember/memorize material	Slow down and reread to retain all details.
Need to correlate with other material	Slow down and mark the text with parallels and contrasts you note.
Need to prepare for a paper, class, discussion, or test	Slow down and pay more attention to details, relationships between and among parts, order of events, etc.; reread as necessary.

The Hunger Games: A Teaching Guide 15

Strategy 2, cont.

Reading Situation	How to Adjust
Difficult vocabulary interfering with comprehension	Pause to use context clues, built-in dictionary, glossary, or outside sources, if necessary.
Long complex or compound sentences	Slow down and note punctuation to ensure that relationships between and among grammatical elements are well understood.
Unfamiliar subject matter	Take enough time when new material is being introduced to absorb it: your grasp of new ideas/concepts/insights will then carry over into the rest of the book.
Complex subject matter	Take extra time and reread when something, by its nature, cannot be easily or clearly described.
Special formatting	Slow down to review charts, maps, graphs, and other illustrations that require more focused study and special interpretation than text.
Varying importance of material	Slow down for more important material, but increase reading rate for less important material.
Varying types of text	Poetry, by its nature, calls for a different type of reading than prose, with attention to sound, for example. Meanings may need to be teased out over a number of readings.

The reading process also depends on the type of text we're reading. Let's imagine texts as existing on a continuum, a range with two endpoints.

efferent (informational) texts───────────────aesthetic (experiential) texts

At one extreme we find **efferent texts**—texts that use words, sentences, and sounds only to convey information, after which the particular words, sentences, and sounds don't matter. It's important that you have the facts, but not important how you acquired them. If what you need to know is whether the king is alive or dead, it does not matter whether the sentence you hear is: "The king is dead" or "The king has passed away" or "The king is no longer with us." In this case, when the content of the message is conveyed, the exact wording of the message no longer matters.

At the continuum's other end, where we find **aesthetic texts**, is poetry, in which the meaning cannot be separated from the particular words, word groups, and sounds the writer chose. In poetry, the sound and sense, along with spelling and grammar and mechanics and usage, are *one* thing, and the experience of these particular choices makes the *one* thing that constitutes the poem for the reader. Information can exist apart from the way it is conveyed; a poem cannot.

In between these two outliers we find narrative fiction—mu h of which belongs in the category of literature. Where on the continuum a particular work of literature, or a particular part of a particular work, lies depends on how it is written. We can only discover its place by the experience itself. But a good approach to literature is to start reading it as if it were written with the care and intentionality of poetry, as if "everything counts."

1. Identify any portions of Chapter 1 for which you altered your reading process and explain what you did and why.

Strategy 3   Marking a Text

Directions: First, read the information. Then, answer the question or questions.

Marking up a text is a good way to make a book your own. You can respond to the author and characters, give yourself helpful reminders, collect information about different parts of the book in one place, and/or record your reactions. Here are some helpful hints on what you can do with either a print or digital edition. If you are reading purely to experience the story, you might not have much (or anything) to say that you want to stop reading for, but if you are reading analytically or to write a paper, you can make your note taking more effective by creating a system.

Book As Conversation

When you read a book, you're engaging with an author who has something to say. By annotating the text, you can speak back. Questions, comments, evaluations, and even arguments are fair game. Some comments you might want to use are:

- But what about . . . ?—for apparent contradictions
- ! (or as many as you need)
- TAT ("think about this")—for points that need pondering
- WM? ("what [does this] mean?")—for points that need clarificatio

Memory Aids

If you know that you will need to find story events, character descriptions, thematic statements, figurative language, etc. again, you can use a variety of techniques to help you relocate what you need:

- Use color—whether with stickies, highlighters, pens, or digital notes—to categorize your comments.
- Close to the front of the book, make lists of page numbers/locations of items you will need to find again: important quotations, appearance of symbols, significant event .
- Invent your own system of margin notes, using symbols to record the occurrence of repetition, symbols, connections, themes, and other important details such as key words or important quotations.

Links/Connections

Sometimes a book will call up a link to another text—a source, reference, or allusion will be known to you; a thought or quotation will connect to something someone else said or wrote. Note it: you may find the connection valuable later. (For more on identifying references and allusions, see Strategy 14, p. 44)

Writing a Paper?

When you're writing a paper, your marginal notes will be only part of what will be useful. In a print edition, flags and self-stick removable notes can be really helpful. If you are searching by chapter, marking each page that begins a chapter with a numbered flag can make locating information much easier than thumbing through every time. You can also color-code your different topics to make your task easier.

1. If you own the copy of *The Hunger Games* that you are reading, use this opportunity to begin developing your own system of text marking. If you don't own the book, invent a system for taking notes in a separate location, in a notebook or on index cards, for example.

The Hunger Games: A Teaching Guide 17

Strategy 4: Plot—Identifying the Overall Design of a Story

Directions: First, read the information. Then, answer the question or questions.

Three-Act Structure

Act One (Setup)
- Inciting Incident X
- Reversal 1 X

Act Two (Confrontation)
- Reversal 2 X

Act Three (Resolution)
- Climax X

People who study and write literature have come up with several different ways of talking about plot. Screenwriters and television script writers arrange their scripts according to a three-part division of beginning, middle, and end, called *acts*. Collins, as a television writer, uses this frame, and we can see that the book is divided into three parts of nine chapters each and is the first part of a trilogy, which has three parts by definition The three-part structure is sometimes represented like this:

1. **Act One**—Set-up, including exposition (background), an *inciting incident* that sets the plot in motion, and a *reversal*, also called a plot point, which moves the action in a new direction.
2. **Act Two**—Confrontation or rising action, including a series of conflicts and ending in a second reversal or plot point
3. **Act Three**—Resolution, including the climax and the tying up of loose ends.

Not every book will have its structure laid out so clearly, but you can still use what information there is to make deductions about its structure. When you begin a book, take a moment to examine what the table of contents and chapter titles indicate about its structure. Make a mental note as you reach significant structure elements (the inciting incident, reversals, etc.), and consider whether overlaying a three-act structure yields insight into the work.

Keep in mind that writers adapt the plot structure for each particular story. They decide how much exposition should be included and where; how many conflicts there will be; what's told to the reader; and what is left for the reader to figure out. In this case, we know something about the way Collins approaches her stories from an interview question:

> **Q: Do you have every book completely mapped out, or do you have a general idea and then take it from there? Did you run into things that were unexpected plot-wise or character-wise?**
>
> A: I've learned it helps me to work out the key structural points before I begin a story. The inciting incident, acts, breaks, mid-story reversal, crisis, climax, those sorts of things. I'll know a lot of what fills the spaces between them as well, but I leave some uncharted room for the characters to develop. And if a door opens along the way, and I'm intrigued by where it leads, I'll definitely go through it
>
> (http://www.scholastic.com/thehungergames/media/suzanne_collins_q_and_q.pdf)

1. As you read *The Hunger Games*, pause at the end of each of the three parts to identify how the plot structure works. When you are done, explain how the story follows and deviates from the three-act structure.

Strategy 5   Identifying the Narrator

A story is always told by someone called the narrator. Usually the narrator of a work of fiction is a **persona** created by the author for the purpose of conveying the story. The narrator may be someone who participates in the action of the story, or someone outside the action of the story. The narrator may have limited knowledge, or may know everything there is to know about the story. The narrator may also be reliable or unreliable. All of these factors go into forming the characteristics of the narrator. The term **point of view** is used to identify one of the important characteristics of a narrator. There are three main viewpoints.

Stories can be told in the **first-person point of view**. In this case, the narrator is usually someone who was present or involved in the action of the story, and this person tells the story using the pronoun *I* to indicate personal involvement. A first-person narrator's perspective is limited by what he or she knows, sees, hears, and is told, as well as any mistakes or misconceptions he or she has. First-person point of view creates a certain kind of intimacy because the narrator is speaking of his or her own experience.

Stories can also be told in the **second-person point of view**, which is distinguished by the fact that the narrator speaks to the reader as *you*, and addresses the reader directly, as if they were speaking together. If the reader understands him- or herself as "you," this creates another type of intimacy: that of a story shaped and styled for this very reader.

The **third-person point of view** is the point of view of a narrator who is separate from the action and tells it from a greater distance than a first-person narrator would. This is the least intimate way of telling a story.

A second- or third-person narrator can be **omniscient**, knowing all the action of the story—even including what is going on in all the characters' minds and knowing what will happen before it happens—or **limited** to only the perspective of one character.

Directions: First, read the information. Then, answer the question or questions.

1. How many words of *The Hunger Games* do you need to read before you can identify the point of view? From what point of view is it told?

2. Identify two passages that show that the narrator is unfolding events as they happen, not telling them from the perspective of the future, looking back on past events.

3. In third-person point of view, the main character—the one from whose perspective the story is told—is often named and described to some degree in a paragraph or several close to the beginning of the book. Explain how the narrator reveals the basic facts about herself in Chapter 1:

    - her name
    - her family members
    - her appearance
    - her age
    - her location

4. What is the narrator's tone or attitude towards the reader? Cite the passages that support your conclusions.

5. How would you describe the personal attributes of the narrator?

The Hunger Games: A Teaching Guide

Chapter 2

The Volunteer; the Boy with the Bread

Vocabulary

blind 21 a structure to conceal hunters
wisp 21 the smallest trace
inhale 21 breathe in
exhale 21 breathe out
stunned 21 so shocked that one cannot think or move
protocol 22 customary/required method
synonymous with 22 means the same as
corpse 22 a dead body of a human being
recognition 22 memory of having seen her before
valor 23 courage; bravery
vaporized 23 exploded into unrecognizable fragments
hysterically 23 w/ uncontrolled emotion
thrashing 23 waving arms and legs wildly
steel 23 prepare one's mind for; brace
trills 23 speaks in a musical way
dissent 24 disagreement
condone 24 approve; give consent
reeks 24 stinks
spunk 24 spirit
admiration 24 respect; warm approval
taunting 24 criticizing in order to get a reaction
plummets 24 falls straight down, very fast
unconscious 24 knocked out; not conscious
trained on 25 aimed at

whisked 25 removed rapidly
warbles 25 sings w/ trills
listed 25 tilted
tenuous 25 fragile
devotion 26 attachment; commitment
interaction 26 mutual exchange
racking 26 torturing; shaking
compensation 26 payment to match value
plaited 27 braided
predicament 27 problematic situation
relentless 28 seemingly unending
threadbare 28 almost worn through
gritty 28 MM abrasive; harsh
keel over 28 fall
regain my feet 28 stand up again
scavenged 29 looked through discards
essentially 29 actually
sodden 29 soaking wet
mesmerized 29 fascinated
luscious 29 sweet and good-smelling
realization 30 new understanding
buckled 30 gave way
weal 30 mark caused by a blow
hearty 31 filling and health
slit 32 cut
spasm 33 sudden, involuntary muscle contraction
anthem 33 a patriotic song

Journal and Discussion Topics

1. Why do you think the Capitol made a way for volunteers to take the place of a child whose name was chosen?
2. As Katniss points out, having the odds in her favor didn't matter for Prim. Given that Effie Trinket's signature line references odds, what inference can you draw about her? Provide other details about Effie Trinket that support your conclusion.
3. Sometimes in first-person narration the narrator has to provide a blow-by-blow account of his or her own actions in order to show what happens. Record examples from Chapter 2 in which Katniss does this.
4. How does Katniss let you know the mayor's background knowledge about her?
5. How soon does Katniss start thinking strategically about the Games? Explain how you know. What practice has she had in the kind of behavior she is practicing now?
6. Considering what Katniss says in Chapter 1 about her lack of friends, she has many connections that, even if they aren't technically friends, are important. List the people she has some kind of relationship with and the reason that the relationship developed.
7. What does Katniss say she'll never know? Why won't she know? Tell your own conclusions about this.
8. What do you think was going on with Katniss's mother after Katniss's father died? Provide evidence to support your conclusion(s).
9. In the first full paragraph on page 28 (beginnin , "Starvation's not . . .," there are several uses of *you* and a question. Describe what's happening in the narration.
10. What evidence is there that Peeta burned the bread on purpose?
11. By the end of the chapter, how is Katniss thinking of Peeta?
12. Summarize the chapter from Peeta's point of view.

20 *The Hunger Games: A Teaching Guide*

Summary

Katniss is shocked that having the odds in one's favor actually does not matter. Prim is already walking up towards the stage, while the crowd murmurs with displeasure that a twelve–year-old has been chosen, when Katniss rushes up, pushes Prim behind her, and volunteers as a tribute. Prim grabs her from behind, screaming that she can't go, but Katniss—intent on not crying so that she will not appear weak—feels Prim being lifted away and turns to see Gale taking Prim back towards her mother. Effie Trinket enthusiastically encourages the crowd to applaud Katniss, but District 12 refuses, first standing in silence, and then giving Katniss their local salute. Just at this moment, Haymitch stumbles across the stage, congratulating Katniss and saying that she has spunk, "more than you!" Whether he is talking to the audience or the camera—and hence the Capitol—is not clear to Katniss because as he shouts, he falls off the stage and knocks himself unconscious.

As Haymitch is taken away on a stretcher, Effie Trinket picks the boy tribute: Peeta Mellark, an ash blond, stocky boy of medium height and son of the town baker. Although prior to the choice, Katniss had been entirely concerned with it not being Gale, she is taken aback when Peeta is chosen. While the mayor reads the Treaty of Treason, Katniss recalls how—when her family was starving in the spring after her father died—she knew she could collect tesserae beginning on her birthday but didn't know if her family would survive till then because they were starving. As she walked down an alley in town checking garbage cans for scraps, the baker's wife came out and yelled at her. As she backed away, Katniss saw Peeta standing in the doorway. Realizing that things were hopeless, Katniss sank to the ground in despair. But then Peeta reemerged with his mother yelling about the loaves having fallen into the fir , calling Peeta names, and telling him to feed the bread to their pig, which he began to do. Katniss noticed a red mark on his cheek, suggesting that his mother hit him for burning the bread. As soon as his mother disappeared, Peeta tossed the loaves toward Katniss and went back into the bakery. She was stunned, but quickly picked them up and took them home, where—with the burnt bits scraped off—they made several meals for her family. She didn't consider until the next morning that Peeta might have purposely spoiled the loaves. But now she also credits him with an epiphany, because that afternoon when she started home after school and caught him staring at her, she looked down in embarrassment, only to see the first dandelion of the year and realize that putting her father's instruction about food plants to use, she had a means to help her family survive. Katniss reflects that she connects Peeta with their survival, and that she has sometimes seen him looking at her at school and feels that she owes him something, perhaps because she never thanked him. Now, she thinks, she never will, because she and Peeta are about to be in a fight to the death, in which context, a thank-you doesn't seem to fit When the mayor finishes the Treaty of Treason, he signals for Peeta and Katniss to shake hands. As they do, she is not sure if Peeta gives her hand a squeeze or has a muscle spasm. The gathering closes with the playing of the anthem of Panem.

Chapter 2, cont.

The Hunger Games: A Teaching Guide 21

Strategy 6

Strategy 6

Interpreting Characterization

Directions: First, read the information. Then, answer the question or questions.

A **character** in a story is someone or something whose actions, choices, thoughts, ideas, words, interactions, and/or influence are important in developing the plot. Characters are often people, but also include other living creatures, and sometimes even non-living things. A force, such as good or evil, can operate as a character in a story.

Most stories have a single character or a small group of characters whose goal or problem is the core of the plot. This character or group of characters is called the **protagonist**. The protagonist does not have to be good, but a good protagonist may be referred to as the "hero" of the story. Readers usually identify with the protagonist and hope that the protagonist will succeed in attaining his or her goal. The character, group, or force, that opposes the protagonist is called the **antagonist**. Especially when the antagonist is a single, evil character, this character may be referred to as the **villain** (see Strategy 16, Plot—Distinguishing Types of Conflict p. 54).

Characters, even those that aren't human, have what we may still call *personality*—a set of characteristic traits and features by which we recognize them. Personality is what helps us distinguish one tribute from another tribute. **Characterization** is the name for the techniques a writer uses to reveal the personality of characters to the reader. Characterization is achieved in a number of different ways, and the use or omission of various techniques can be revealing.

- **Words:** dialogue about the character, as well as the character's own words and how they are said—dialect, slang, and tone—are important; what is *not* said can also be important
- **Thoughts:** what's going on in the character's mind, and the character's motives
- **Appearance:** the character's physical characteristics, clothing, and accessories (these may be symbolic; for example, Prim's untucked shirt suggests that she's childlike and innocent)
- **Action:** what the character does
- **Choices**: the decisions the character makes
- **Interactions:** how the character relates to others
- **Names:** often symbolic of a major character trait or role (see Strategy 11: Interpreting Names p. 35)
- **Chosen Setting:** the furnishings, etc., with which the character chooses to surround him- or herself
- **Change/Development:** the occurrence of and direction of change or development that a character undergoes

1. What techniques are used in Chapter 2 to characterize Peeta? Prim?
2. How do the verbs of speaking (synonyms of *said*) that Katniss uses for Effie Trinket help to characterize her?
3. Describe the character of Peeta's mother and tell what evidence led to your conclusions.
4. Katniss says a few things about what she imagines will and won't happen in her future interactions with Peeta. How does this reflect on her? What evidence suggests that Peeta is thinking differently?
5. Can you identify a protagonist and antagonist in this story? Explain.

Strategy 7

Plot—Foreshadowing and Flashback

Directions: First, read the information. Then, answer the question or questions.

Writers do not always tell plot events in chronological order. Here, we're going to focus on two ways events may be out of order. First, the story may hint at events before their place in the sequence. This is called **foreshadowing**, and it lets readers know beforehand something about what is going to happen later. This technique helps create suspense and keeps the reader involved in the unfolding plot.

Foreshadowing may come from the book title or a chapter title, from a character's words, from the setting, or from the narrator. The title of this book is a very straightforward foreshadowing of the key event in the novel: the Games for which the reaping is providing "players." Foreshadowing can also be provided by a character's predictions (such as Katniss's about hers and Peeta's expected interactions in the arena), a change of setting, or the narrator's comment (when the narrator is not a character).

With the focus in this book on a fight to the death, it is likely that the foreshadowing will be kept fairly subtle to prevent giving away too much and undermining suspense, while still creating a strong basis for later actions, choices, and events.

A second way that writers may alter the timeline is to include material that happened prior to the beginning of the story or earlier in the plot sequence. When the material is already known to the reader and the writer is repeating it, the repetition is called **recap**. Since recap depends on being farther into a story, we won't see any this early in the book. When this material is new to the reader, it is often called **flashback**, and it is frequently part of the exposition of the novel, providing essential background information (see Strategy 4: Plot—Identifying the Overall Design of a Story, p. 18) either at the beginning of the novel or later.

Flashbacks may come from the narrator or the characters and may be more or less important. With the protagonist as the first-person narrator, the source of most of the flashbacks is likely to be Katniss. Her first flashback comes on the very first page, when she recounts how the family acquired their cat. Given this early flashback and the nature of the story, in which the history of the country and the history of interactions between and among characters is important, it's safe to expect that more flashbacks will be used to explain the current situation to readers.

As you read other works, you may find it revealing to pause once in awhile and consider the timeline and whether chronological order is being strictly adhered to or interrupted with foreshadowing of things to come or flashbacks of material that occurred in an earlier time frame. The purpose and frequency of these alterations in order can help you understand more about a book's structure.

1. Make a list of all the flashbacks in the first two chapters. Identify how each one increases your understanding of the situation and the characters.

The Hunger Games: A Teaching Guide 23

Strategy 8 — Analyzing Choices

Directions: First, read the information. Then, answer the question or questions.

Here is a 4-part Choice Analysis Tool to use in understanding choices in *The Hunger Games*. Part 1 is for analyzing the situation, Part 2 for analyzing motivation (why people make the choices they do), Part 3 for analyzing the decision maker's access to reliable information, and Part 4 for analyzing the finality of the hoice.

1. Select one or more appropriate items from each part to characterize:
   a. Katniss's choice to volunteer for Prim
   b. Peeta's choices that resulted in Katniss and her family having bread
   c. Katniss's and Gale's choice to hunt, fish and gather

PART 1—TYPES OF CHOICES

Free Choice (Voluntary)

A decision with no limitations or constraint from anyone or anything

- A *pet owner* decides to name her gerbil *Wally*, rather than *Rudolfus*.

Offer (Voluntary)

A decision in which some alternative possibility with no strings or pressure is considered and freely chosen

- A *commuter* accepts a ride from a neighbor headed in the same direction rather than walk.

Constrained Choice (Voluntary within the constrained circumstances)

A decision in which there is some limitation caused by resources or the situation (such as money, time, other peoples' taste), but no threat

- A *teen* watches a movie online instead of going to the theatre. ($/time/transportation)

Bargain (Voluntary)

A decision in which two or more people come to a mutual agreement without threat, and with or without compromise

- A *man* agrees to lunch with a colleague who has a 2-for-1 deal at an expensive restaurant on the understanding that they will split the bill.

Choice w/ Spelled-Out Consequences (Voluntary)

A decision in which choices are curtailed by the consequences, which may be arbitrary, but do not violate the decision-maker's rights and are presented as fact, not threat

- A *woman* having a garage sale wants to sell a CD for $8. A shopper says she won't spend more than $6 for it.

Exploitive Choice (Either Voluntary-Under-the-Circumstances or Involuntary)

A choice is offered that takes advantage of a power differential and the fact that the chooser is not in a position to bargain.

- A *person* with no unemployment benefits and no other job prospects is offered a job for wages that are less that the value of his labor.

Coerced Choice (Either Voluntary-Under-the-Circumstances or Involuntary)

A decision that is influenced by a credible threat, with the consequence for non-compliance being unwelcome and violating the coerced person's rights/freedom.

- A *person* is told by a blackmailer to pay a certain sum or the illegal thing the person did will be shared with the police.

Terrorized Choice (Either Voluntary-Under-the-Circumstances or Involuntary)

A decision that is not only influenced by a credible threat that violates the person's rights and is unwelcome, but is made more credible by the fact that harm has or is currently being caused or physical force is being used, so that the person's rights/freedom are already violated in unwelcome ways.

- A *person* being held hostage is commanded to rob a bank or lose his/her life.

24   *The Hunger Games: A Teaching Guide*

PART 2—MOTIVATIONS/INTENTIONS/DESIRES

Seeking a good for oneself

Life
- Food and Water
- Shelter
- Safety
- Sleep
- Health/Healthcare
- Equality

Liberty
- Freedom from coercion and terrorism
- Rational, predictable, fair, honest treatment by the state
- Justice
- Self-Direction

Happiness
- Become Educated
- Achieve Accomplishments
    - (e.g., Attain Physical Prowess, Succeed in a Career, Attain and Exercise Authority)
- Acquire and Own Property
- Gain Status Corresponding to Accomplishments
- Enjoy Love/Friendship/Family
- Express one's Feelings
- Create Beauty
- Reach a Satisfied Emotional Stat
    - (e.g., Take a Vacation, Go for a Walk in Nature)
- Enjoy Entertainment
- Build Community

Seeking a good for specific other person

Same as good for self, more or less

Seeking a good for the community

Same as good for self, more or less

Seeking a Theoretical Good

Doing the right thing by practicing a virtue or following a rule, law, or belief

Keeping a promise or fulfilling another type of obligation or responsibilit

(Any of the above can be carried out to excess/immoderately, illegally, or with disregard for others or to the detriment of others; some can be carried out inadequately.)

PART 3—INFORMATION LEVEL AND AWARENESS

Level of Information

No Information
Partial Information
Complete Information

Awareness of Level of Information

Aware
Partially Aware
Unaware
Mistaken in awareness of level

Quality of Information

True
False
   Misinformation
   Lies
   Invalid Conclusions
   Wishful Thinking

PART 4—EXTENT OF CHOICE

Final Choice

Non-Final Choice

  Choice Made in Stages
  Retracted Choice
  Revised Choice

Strategy 8, cont.

The Hunger Games: A Teaching Guide

Writer's Forum 1

Writing a News Story

Directions: First, read the information. Then, answer the question or questions.

A news article, whether for a print newspaper or online delivery, generally aims to give an objective report of an event that is important to the people who read that particular paper or website. While the event can be local, national, or international, it must have some impact on or hold some interest for the readership.

The headline of a news article both catches the reader's attention and declares the main topic of the article. Sports or feature articles may have a cryptic headline—one that asks a question that the article will answer, or one that includes wordplay—to get the reader interested, but strict news headlines are usually straightforward.

Headlines are distinguished from regular sentences by having all their important words (first and last word, nouns, pronouns, verbs, adjectives, and adverbs) capitalized. Because headlines are shown in large type, they often take shortcuts, skipping words that you would expect to see in prose in order to fit the space. So, a general news story headline about the 74th reaping of tributes might be something like one of these:

Reaping Harvests 24 Tributes for the 74th Hunger Games

Most Volunteers Ever in Today's Reaping

Tributes Ages 12 to 18 Chosen on 74th Reaping Day

The first paragraph of a news article gives the reader a quick summary of the important details, usually by telling the 5 W's (Who, What, Where, When, and Why) and How. Subsequent paragraphs give additional details that fill out the story. The first paragraph of a news story taking an overall view of the reaping might read like this:

> Today's reaping, the 74th in Panem history, yielded the requisite 24 tributes—a boy and a girl from each of our 12 Districts—to participate in the upcoming Hunger Games, to be held in the arena at an undisclosed location. As always, there can be only one winner, a boy or girl who will secure a life of ease for him- or herself and plentiful gifts for his or her district, and sponsors are eager to meet this year's contenders.

News stories often include material gathered from interviews. This material may be stated directly as quotations or indirectly. Proper capitalization and punctuation should be used in any quotations (see Writer's Forum 3: Writing Dialogue, p. 50 for a guide)

> Direct quotation: "I volunteer!" cried Katniss Everdeen
> Indirect quotation: Katniss Everdeen said that she volunteered.

1. You are a news reporter from the Capitol. Write a news story about the reaping in District 12. You may make up supporting information to add details to the story, but make sure they're true to the story and are the kinds of thing a reporter would be able to find out The news story should include at least one quotation. Give yourself a byline, and make your story look like a news article. You may include an illustration with a caption if you wish.

Chapter 3

Goodbyes; Trip to the Capitol Begins

Chapter 3 Page 34

Vocabulary

pact 35 formal agreement
clock out 35 fail to be present/engaged; from punching out after a workday
abandonment 35 withdrawal
immobilizing 36 crippling; disabling
insurmountable 36 unable to be overcome
plush 37 w/ expensive, lush fabric
evasive 38 attempting to avoid something
urgency 38 insistence
maces 39 club-shaped weapons w/ spiked metal heads
bludgeon 39 club
insane 39 out of one's mind; unbalanced
anticlimactic 39 ineffective as storytelling
swarming 40 overrun
sniveling 41 always crying and whining
viciously 41 maliciously; nastily
mercifully 41 to my great relief
sanctioned 41 approved or permitted by authority
blather 42 meaningless talk; babble
at [one's] disposal 42 available for one's use
bred 42 brought into being
genetically 42 in their gene
altered 42 changed
exclusively 43 only
replicate 43 copy
enunciate 43 speak clearly
savages 44 uncivilized people
digestion 44 breaking down food
purse 45 contract lips to show disapproval
concoction 45 something made from a combination of ingredients
lunges 45 throws oneself
demeanor 45 the way one looks, holds oneself, and acts
decrepit 46 broken down
on cue 46 scripted; planned
disgruntled 46 upset; indignant
mentor 46 wise, guiding counselor
smirking 46 smiling w/ contempt
dictates 46 controls

Journal and Discussion Questions

1. Katniss could theoretically tell her mother and Prim some things simply because she is going away; some because of her particular role in the family; and some because she doesn't expect to ever see them again. Categorize her statements to them into these three categories.
2. What realities are against Katniss's chances of winning the Hunger Games?
3. Given the facts of their lives, what do you think are the most important things for people in District 12 to know, understand, and be able to do? Does the education system provide opportunities for them to learn these things? Explain your answer.
4. What do you think was the baker's motivation for visiting Katniss?
5. What details make Madge seem very determined to ensure that Katniss takes and wears her pin? Offer at least one explanation for why Madge should be so determined about this.
6. Do you think Gale gives Katniss valuable advice? Explain.
7. In this chapter, what does Katniss say she'll never know?
8. What do you think Gale's last words were?
9. After looking more closely at the pin Madge gave her, how does Katniss interpret it? Why? What other interpretation(s) is/are possible?
10. Why is it significant that Peeta had been crying?
11. Which aspects of Katniss's experience in this chapter could be described by the word *opulence*?
12. How is the use of the word *savages* important?
13. What does the phrase "as if on cue" suggest about Haymitch's action? If the action was "on cue," what do you think it means?
14. According to Effie Trinket, why should Peeta and Katniss reconsider their stance that Haymitch's drunken antics are amusing?
15. Summarize this chapter from the point of view of one of the Peacekeepers who accompanied and guarded Katniss from the stage to (presumably) the train.

The Hunger Games: A Teaching Guide

Chapter 3, cont.

Summary

As the anthem ends, District 12's two tributes are escorted into the Justice Building by Peacekeepers, and placed in separate, expensively-furnished rooms to say goodbye to family and friends. Katniss is first visited by her mother and Prim. While Prim sits on her lap, Katniss tries to pass on all her wisdom on how they can stay alive with the proceeds from their mother's fledgling apothecary business and Prim's goat, and by trading with Gale for medicinal herbs and game. But then she grabs her mother and insists that she mustn't allow her depression to take over. Mrs. Everdeen defensively says that if she had the medicine she now has, she could have cured herself. Prim asks Katniss to promise that she'll "really, really" try to win, and although she doesn't believe it's possible, Katniss promises. As the Peacekeeper indicates that time is up, she hugs them and says, "I love you."

Katniss's next visitor is, unexpectedly, Peeta Mellark's father. He gives her cookies, and promises to make sure Prim has enough to eat. The third visitor, also a surprise, is Madge, who insists on giving Katniss her gold pin, which shows a small bird, making her promise to wear it into the arena as her token from her district. Madge kisses her cheek, and Katniss wonders if Madge is more of a friend than Katniss had given her credit for.

Gale, her last visitor, comes in and gives her a hug. He advises her above all to get or make a bow. Gale reminds her that the Games are "just hunting" and that she knows how to kill. Katniss points out that she has never killed a person, and Gale responds, "How different can it be, really?" As the Peacekeepers force him to leave, Katniss begs Gale to make sure her family doesn't starve, and he affirms that he will, telling her to "remember I__" before the door closes, cutting off his words.

The tributes are taken to a Capitol-bound train, which is surrounded by reporters, making Katniss glad she hasn't cried. She notices that Peeta has wept and makes no attempt to hide it. She considers what this strategy might imply and recalls that Johanna Mason, a tribute from District 7, faked weakness and went on to become a victor. On the train, Katniss goes to her sumptuous quarters, where she examines Madge's pin, now recognizing that it shows a mockingjay, a cross between the Capitol's abandoned genetically-altered birds called *jabberjays* and "normal" mockingbirds. The Capitol used jabberjays—which could memorize and repeat human conversation—to collect intelligence about citizens, but stopped the experiment when the districts figured it out and began feeding them false information. Katniss's father was fond of mockingjays, which retained the ability to memorize and repeat, but could only do it with music and would echo songs he sang. Katniss, therefore, associates the pin with her father.

At supper, Effie Trinket, Peeta, and Katniss gather. Haymitch is absent from dinner and from the broadcast afterwards in which the reapings of all 12 districts are shown, providing Katniss's and Peeta's first sighting of their competition. Katniss is haunted by the 12-year-old girl from District 11, who has dark skin but reminds her of Prim. As they watch their own reaping in District 12, Effie Trinket criticizes Haymitch, and Peeta laughingly points out that Haymitch was drunk, as he is at the reaping every year, which Katniss jokingly amends to "every day." Effie Trinket mocks their attitude, telling them that as their mentor, Haymitch is their lifeline. Haymitch staggers in just then, vomits, and falls into the mess. Effie le ves, making a snide remark.

Strategy 9 — Setting and Mood

Directions: First, read the information. Then, answer the question or questions.

Setting refers to both the world in which the story takes place and the changing scenery that serves as the backdrop for each scene or chapter. Setting includes what the characters can sense in their environment, e.g.,

- time of day
- season of the year
- plants and animals
- natural features
- weather
- landscape
- buildings or other structures
- human-made features

The general setting of this story is Panem, a country that covers what's left of North America at some time in the future. The story begins in Chapter 1 with several specific locales within Panem: Katniss's family home in District 12, the woods beyond the fence, and the town square.

Setting may be a mere backdrop to the story, or it can serve other functions, sometimes even several different functions within one story. Setting often contributes to characterization, when characters are able to choose aspects of their setting (see Strategy 6, p. 22). For example, from reading the description of the special place that she and Gale share in the woods on p. 6, we gain some insight into Katniss's character.

Setting may also be symbolic (the town square as the community meeting place) or create conflicts for the characters, hindering the characters in achieving their goal(s), or creating physical hardships or challenges that are difficult to overcome. Setting can also provide materials or resources that help the characters solve problems.

The settings of a story and how the settings function affect how we and the characters feel about their surroundings. This feeling is called **mood**. The setting can make things seem pleasant or create an air of foreboding that hints that something bad is about to happen, or convey many other moods. For example, the description of the chain-link fence with barbed wire on top that surrounds District 12 on p. 4 may seem a bit chilling to the reader, though Katniss—having lived with it all her life—takes it in stride.

Although a novel like *The Hunger Games* is classified as a narrative—a type of writing that tells a story—sections of a novel that deal with the setting are usually passages of description. You may be aware of the shift back and forth from narrative to description as you read.

As you read descriptions of setting, try to figure out what Collins (or any other author) is aiming to convey. Paying attention to the possibilities and problems created by the setting and the mood these functions creates will help you reach a deeper understanding.

1. Extend the following chart to create a record of *The Hunger Games* settings and their functions by skimming the chapters you've already read and continuing to add as you read more.

Chapter	Setting Description	Function(s) in Story	Mood Created
1			
2			
...			

The Hunger Games: A Teaching Guide

Chapter 4

**Chapter 4
Page 48**

Tributes Confront Haymitch; Arrival at the Capitol

Vocabulary

vile 48 disgusting
good impression 48 positive impact
revenge 49 repayment for an injury
scrounged 50 foraged scarce resources
gorged 50 ate greedily until completely full
roused 51 came out of a state of inactivity
carcass 51 dead body of an animal
savior 51 something that rescues or saves
edible 51 safe to eat
inexplicable 51 unable to be explained
gnarled 53 twisted and distorted
deteriorated 54 fell apart; became worse
oblivion 54 a state of being unaware

stylist 55 person who coordinates another's appearance
obscenities 55 foul language
indulgences 55 excessive consumption
tureen 55 large, covered dish to hold soup
beckons 55 calls; invites
incoherent 56 unclear; confused
deflect 57 turn away; turn aside
cornucopia 58 horn holding endless food and drink
grandeur 59 ability to arouse admiration
glistening 59 shining
hues 59 colors
gawking 60 staring too long and intently

Journal and Discussion Questions

1. What narrative function does throwing the cookies out the window serve?
2. What combination of factors saved Katniss's family from starvation?
3. Offer a defense for Haymitch from Katniss's analysis of why she detests him.
4. Why does Haymitch's level of engagement suddenly change?
5. Use the Choice Analysis Tool to analyze the choice Haymitch offers the tributes.
6. *Character foils* are characters who represent opposing points of view or ways of life. Identify any character foils that Collins has introduced.
7. Katniss presents strikingly different views of Peeta at different times. Respond to her two evaluations of Peeta's motivations, and offer your own interpretation.
8. How does the Capitol benefit from h ving two tributes/district, rather than one?
9. How do Katniss's observations about her first sighting of the Capitol expand on her previous comments about the Capitol and its citizens?

Summary

Katniss and Peeta help Haymitch to his compartment and into his bathtub, and turn on the shower. Peeta offers to take care of him, and refuses Katniss's offer to call one of the Capitol attendants. Katniss reconsiders Peeta's motivation, concluding that he really is kind, thus a threat to her because she's drawn to kind people, but can't afford to feel affection for Peeta in the circumstances. Attempting to shut down her feelings about him, she throws the cookies out the train window. They land by a patch of dandelions, leading Katniss back to the flashba k begun in Chapter 2. Realizing she could use plants for food, she took Prim to the Meadow to collect dandelions. Then she found her mother's book of medicinal plants, into which their father had added entries for food plants. The next day, Katniss made her first illegal foray beyond the fence without her father, and the woods became the family's "savior," as Katniss hunted, gathered, and built up a trade. By then, their mother had recovered. But although Prim forgave her immediately, Katniss never fully trusted her. Katniss is saddened by the thought that she can never set this right, but then recalls saying she loved her mother at the Justice Building, and hopes this will serve. Preparing for sleep, Katniss thinks of her mother and Prim.

She is awakened by Effie Trinket and eats a large breakfast, while Haymitch adds spirits to his juice. Realizing that she detests him, she confronts him. Peeta joins in, breaking the glass holding the alcohol. Haymitch punches Peeta in the jaw, whereupon Katniss drives a knife into the table between the bottle and Haymitch's hand. Haymitch begins to question them about their abilities, sizes them up, and makes a deal with them to stay sober enough to help them if they do exactly what he says. They agree. His first order is to allow their stylists to do whatever they want, without resisting. As he leaves the car, it goes dark because the train has entered the mountains that separate the Capitol from the districts in the east. Returning light reveals the splendor of the Capitol. As spectators begin to point at them, Katniss withdraws, but Peeta smiles and waves, saying that one of them may prove to be a valuable sponsor. This leads Katniss to conclude that she misjudged him, and that he is not kind, but determined to live, and therefore a deadly threat to her in a different way than she had thought.

30 *The Hunger Games: A Teaching Guide*

Strategy 10   Forming Hypotheses

Directions: First, read the information. Then, answer the question or questions.

Making predictions is a normal part of reading. And leading (and misleading) the reader's expectations is something that all good writers do. As readers, we make predictions about causes, results, and intentions. These predictions could be based on various things, such as a gut feeling or what we wish were true. It is only when we base a prediction on evidence that it merits the name of **hypothesis**.

Some people associate the word *hypothesis* strictly with scientific investigation. But that is not the limit of its application. Readers are constantly making and testing hypotheses about characters' reasons for their choices and actions, about what will happen next in the plot, about what is true in the world of the story, and about the author's intentions. Here are some criteria for a good hypothesis.

- **A good hypothesis should be of significance in the world of the story.** If we were reading a journal article on the science of nutrition, the apparent rarity of citrus fruit in District 12 would be of some significanc . But in *The Hunger Games*, it's not important beyond helping to establish the stunning difference between standards of living in various parts of Panem. Katniss's ability to think analyze her own and others' choices, on the other hand, is likely to be essential in her performance in the Games and should hold some interest and focus for the reader. It seems apparent that Collins is carefully shaping the material to create suspense about Katniss's ability to interpret other peoples' motivations.

- **A good hypothesis should be clearly stated and specific so that you can easily tell what it means**, **but it should reach beyond what you know for certain**. If you formed the hypothesis, *Maybe Katniss's ability to read others will prove important*, it would not do you any good. That Katniss's insight is important in this story is something we have already established. A hypothesis is a statement about which you do not yet know the truth.

- **A good hypothesis should identify the motivation, result, or intention that you think you have identified**. For example, having seen Katniss's changing opinions of Peeta and her suspicions about Haymitch, we might wonder whether Katniss's wavering on the conclusions she draws will prove damaging to her chances of winning the Games. Given the evidence, you might form the following hypothesis: *Maybe Katniss's ability to understand other people's motivations will grow through trial and error as she goes through the experience of the Games*. Once you form a hypothesis, you should look for further information to verify or disprove it.

1. Form a hypothesis about Katniss, Peeta, Haymitch, the tributes in the broadcast who stood out to Katniss, how the results of the game will work (or not) in the Capitol's favor, or some other important part of the story. Collect and record evidence from Chapters 1–4 that supports your hypothesis. Write your hypothesis and explain the evidence that supports it. You may wish to arrange the evidence in the order of decreasing importance (most important point first) or increasing importance (most important point last). You'll get a chance to review your hypothesis in Strategy 20 (p. 73).

The Hunger Games: A Teaching Guide

Writer's Forum 2

Comparing and Contrasting

Directions: First, read the information. Then, answer the question or questions.

Comparing and contrasting puts two or more subjects side by side in order to draw insights from their similarities and differences. In a compare and contrast essay, you show the similarities and differences between people, things, ideas, approaches, etc., and draw some conclusion based on your examination. You choose the categories to compare and contrast based on your purpose and subject.

For example, if you were comparing and contrasting Peeta's father and mother, you might choose categories such as "work," "relationship to Peeta," "relationship to Katniss and her family," " For different subjects, you would choose different categories. A Venn diagram or other graphic organizer can help you organize the information you will use. A Venn diagram shows visually what two or more subjects have in common and what characteristics they have independently that they do not share.

Here is an example:

only Mr. Mellark   common traits   only Mrs. Mellark

There are two standard ways of organizing a compare and contrast essay. In the **point-by-point method**, you mention each category and all the information about it for both of the things you are considering. For the category "relationship to Katniss and her family," you might write:

> Mr. Mellark often trades with Katniss and brings her cookies before she leaves for the games, promising to look after Prim. In contrast, Mrs. Mellark refuses to feed Katniss and her family when they are starving, and shows no interest in Prim's well-being.

In the other style of organization, the **block method**, you would first cover every category for one of the things you are considering, and then the other. So, for example, you would say everything you had to say about Mr. Mellark and then everything you had to say about Mrs. Mellark, or vice versa. In either case, these words to express similarity and difference are often useful:

Similarity

alike	as well as	furthermore	resemble
also	at the same time	in addition	similarly
and	besides	likewise	too

Difference

but	however	though
conversely	on the contrary	whereas
differ	on the other hand	while

1. Make a list of the categories you would use to compare and contrast District 12 with the Capitol.
2. Write an essay comparing and contrasting Effie and H ymitch.

32   *The Hunger Games: A Teaching Guide*

Chapter 5   Cinna Creates a Girl on Fire

Vocabulary

clipped words 61 words for which the ending is not pronounced, like *dunno* for *don't know* (the *t* is clipped, i.e., not pronounced)
sympathetic 61 showing concern for someone else's pain or discomfort
swathe 61 strip of wrapping material, like a bandage (typo—should be *swath*: broad strip of something)
gritty 61 MM having small, rough particles
primarily 61 mainly
ridding of 61 freeing from
vulnerable 62 able to be hurt
corkscrew 62 having a spiral shape
wielding 62 ready to employ
self-conscious 62 strongly aware of the impression one is making on others
impulse 63 urge; desire
taken aback 63 surprised and put off guard
surgically 63 through a medical operation
concession 63 giving in; yielding
hideous 63 ugly
affectations 63 artificial beh vior meant to impress
flamboyant 64 outrageously showy
expectations 64 ideas about what's going to happen or how things will be
desirable 64 wanted; wished for

combing 65 searching intently
despicable 65 deserving of contempt
complementary 66 completing each other
jumpsuits 66 one-piece suits that covers the entire body for protetction
skimpy 66 short and revealing a lot of skin
stark 66 bare
unforgettable 66 very likely to be remembered
synthetic 67 made by people; not natural
relatively 67 more or less
revelation 67 sudden realization
giddy 67 excited but w/out seriousness
petrified 68 terrifie
tunics 69 garment like a coat w/ a short skirt; may or may not have sleeves
ignites 69 sets on fir
ablaze 69 on fir
illuminates 70 shines on
utterly 70 completely
suppress 70 hold back; control
flicker 70 a slight sensation; flutte
tangible 71 concrete; able to be touched
regains 71 takes possession of again
prestigious 71 honored or esteemed
engulfed 72 surrounded by
extinguishes 72 puts out flame
luring 72 attracting w/ intent to harm

Journal and Discussion Questions

1. Judging by the descriptions of the prep team and their preparation of Katniss, what are the standards of beauty in the Capitol?
2. What do you make of Flavius's praise of Katniss's appearance post-prep and her response?
3. In what ways is Katniss's styling degrading? In what ways is it well-intentioned?
4. Compare Katniss's thoughts about her mother in Chapter 5 to the way she thought about her in Chapter 3?
5. What mistaken assumption does Katniss make about Cinna? Why is this error important?
6. What do you imagine could have been Cinna's motivation for requesting District 12?
7. What is the narrative function of the meal Katniss shares with Cinna?
8. Were you surprised when Cinna said he would dress Katniss and Peeta in complementary costumes? Why or why not?
9. Why is it important for Katniss to be recognizable in the arena?
10. Why do you think Cinna wanted Katniss and Peeta to hold hands?
11. How does the crowd's response to Katniss and Peeta change during the course of their ride?
12. What is your first impression of the president of anem?
13. Do you think Katniss is right in her analysis of what's behind Peeta's comment and smile?
14. What does Katniss mean when she says "two can play at this game"?
15. Summarize the chapter from Cinna's point of view.

The Hunger Games: A Teaching Guide   33

Chapter 5, cont.

Summary

In the Training Center, Katniss is being prepared by three members of a Capitol prep team (Venia, Octavia, and Flavius) and reflecting on Capitol culture, as represented by the team. As they remove hair from her body, she derides their accent, appearance, and attitudes. Nevertheless, she plays along, winning their affection by the time they call her stylist, Cinna, and she recognizes that they are sincere in their efforts to help her. Touching her still-braided hair, she recalls that she left her mother's dress on the floor of the train, leaving her nothing to connect her with her mother and home: she wishes she'd held onto it.

When Cinna arrives, she is startled to hear his unaffected voice and see that he looks very normal. Katniss asks if he is new, assuming that this is why he was saddled with District 12, but he responds that he is new and he requested District 12. He invites her to discuss preparations for the opening ceremonies this coming evening. They will feature each pair of tributes riding in a horse-drawn chariot, wearing costumes reflecting their district. As they share a meal (which Katniss calculates could only be poorly reproduce in District 12, even with an enormous amount of work), she wonders what Capitol people do with all their time, besides indulging in body art and waiting for tributes to die as entertainment. Cinna, seeming to read her, says that the Capitol must seem despicable to her.

Cinna then explains that his partner, Portia, is Peeta's stylist and that they plan to dress the two in complementary costumes. Katniss recalls the terrible past choices for District 12, but Cinna and Portia intend to represent coal by featuring fire, having created costumes in which simple black unitards are supplemented with capes and headpieces that will burn with synthetic flame. At the same time, they plan to use minimal makeup and preserve Katniss's usual down-the-back braid so that Katniss and Peeta will be recognizable in the arena and spectators will connect Katniss with the "girl on fire."

When they mount the chariot, Katniss and Peeta, concerned about the safety of the fire, make a pact to tear off each other's capes, if necessary. Cinna lights their capes and headdresses, and just before they set off, makes a signal that Peeta sees means for them to hold hands, which they do. Soon, the spectators begin chanting "District 12!" and Katniss grows excited, beginning to feel a little hope that she might gain a sponsor who would help her win the Games. She responds to the crowd, waving and blowing kisses, as the chants shift to her name.

Realizing how tightly she's been holding Peeta's hand, Katniss relaxes her fingers when they reach the City Circle, but he asks her to hold on to help keep him from falling off, and she complies. As the parade stops before the balcony of President Snow while the national anthem plays, Katniss observes that the live coverage, shown on a screen, is giving her chariot far more attention than the others. When they return to the Training Center, they are mobbed by their prep teams, but Katniss notices the dirty looks they are receiving from the other tributes. Portia puts out the flame, and Peeta compliments Katniss in a sweet way that makes her want to respond. But remembering her conclusion that Peeta plans to win, she reinterprets this as strategic rather than genuine, and—deciding that she can act strategically, too—kisses his cheek where it is bruised from Haymitch's punch.

Strategy 11 Interpreting Names

Directions: First, read the information. Then, answer the question or questions.

Character names and place names can simply be names, or they can be descriptive or symbolic, carrying an extra layer of meaning. The use of unusual names and the anecdote about Katniss's name in Chapter 4 seem designed to draw attention to characters' names, so it seems appropriate to examine them in this book. Some people have made exhaustive searches and linked the character names to every possible source. But this is not necessarily fruitful. The key is to find patterns and meanings that augment the meaning of the book, not just collect possibilities.

Sometimes authors use a single scheme, but Collins treats character names in several different ways. Let's take them in groups and see if we can establish any meaningful patterns.

The names of five residents of the Capitol—*Venia, Octavia, Flavius, Cinna,* and *Portia*—as well as the country itself—*Panem*—all come from Latin. Collins has said that *Panem* comes from the Latin saying "panem et circenses" - literally "bread and circuses" - a criticism of the Roman government, which provided food and entertainment to the Roman people in order to prevent discontent (http://www.scholastic.com/thehungergames/media/suzanne_collins_q_and_q.pdf). It is easy to see how the Games in Panem may have parallels with the games of Ancient Rome, and Collins has said that she based the Hunger Games on gladiatorial combat.

The other Latin names have less certain connections. One might think that the fact that *Venia* can mean "indulgence" is suggestive of Venia's character or that the poet named Helvius Cinna who wrote about metamorphosis (changing forms) could link to Cinna's role as a costume designer, but beyond that, it's hard to say.

The name *Effie Trinket* is not Latin, and—for now—stands alone. *Effie* is a nickname for the Greek given name *Euphemia*, which means "well-spoken." Given her public speaking at the reaping, it seems that this may be ironic (for more on irony, see Strategy 21, p. 78). A *trinket* is a small ornament of little value, and this might reflect on her focus on the trivial. As of this chapter, it remains to be seen if a pattern will develop.

The names of the most important characters from District 12 have a strong link to nature and food. Collins has said that *Everdeen* comes from Bathsheba Everdene, a farmer with multiple suitors in Thomas Hardy's novel *Far From the Madding Crowd*. (http://shelf-life.ew.com/2010/08/12/suzanne-collins-on-the-books-she-loves/) Besides this, *Katniss* and *Primrose* are both plants—one used for food and one whose flowers are prized. *Buttercup* is also a flower name). *Madge* is short for *Margaret*, which means "pearl"; *hay* (as in *Haymitch*) is a crop; *Peeta*, the baker, is pronounced like *pita*, a form of bread; *lark* (as in *Mellark*) is a bird; and *Gale* is a strong wind.

In a different vein, Madge's surname is *Undersee*, which may relate to her father's position as mayor - he *oversees* the District, but he is *under* the authority of the Capitol.

When you read a book in which names seem meaningful, explore further, keeping in mind that there may be multiple naming schemes used.

1. As you continue reading,
   a. look for names of Panem residents that are either from Latin or refer to things that are trivial, unimportant, or without lasting value;
   b. look for names of District residents that come from nature

The Hunger Games: A Teaching Guide 35

Chapter 6 — The Avox

Vocabulary

exhilarating 73 exciting
corral 73 collect and direct to
chaperoned 73 supervised
complimentary 74 offering praise
barbarism 74 uncivilized condition
slaughter 74 brutal or violent killing
reservations 74 doubts; misgivings
presided over 75 overseen
civilizing 76 making less savage or rude
deftly 77 skillfully
porcelain 77 pale and perfect, like a doll
utter 77 say aloud
unease 77 anxiety or discomfort
traitor 77 one who betrays his/her country
debut 78 first public appearanc

adversaries 79 opponents; enemies
distinguished 79 set apart from others
maimed 80 impaired; missing a part
under surveillance 80 being watched
immobilized 82 made (us) unable to move
at bay 82 forced to turn and face predators because fleeing is no longer an optio
hovercraft 82 aircraft that can hold its position in the air
secures 83 fastens
toxic 83 poisonous
prime 83 first-rat
contemplating 84 thinking about
mutilate 85 injure; disfigur

Journal and Discussion Questions

1. Look up the prefix *a-* and the root word *vox* to find the literal meaning for *Avox*.
2. Explain how Peeta covers for two missteps in the chapter, Katniss's and his own.
3. Do you think Katniss correctly analyzes why Haymitch admires the hand-holding? Why do you think Portia, rather than Cinna, answers Haymitch's question?
4. What lie does Katniss tell Peeta? Why does she lie?
5. List the four regrets that Katniss has mentioned.
6 Summarize the chapter from the Avox's point of view including how she might have remembered the event that led Katniss to identify her.

Summary

Katniss and Peeta are shown to their quarters in the Training Center. Dinner is served by silent young men and women in white tunics, one of whom Katniss suddenly recognizes, blurting out, "... oh! I know you!" Effie snaps at her for thinking she could know an "Avox," but Katniss doesn't recognize the term. Haymitch define *Avox* as someone who's committed a crime, likely treason, and had his or her tongue cut out, to which Effie adds that one is only to speak to them to give orders. Peeta jumps in, saying that the Avox looks just like Delly Cartwright, someone Katniss knows as well and which is patently untrue. Realizing that Peeta is covering for her, Katniss agrees. Everybody relaxes, and they eat cake and watch the broadcast of the opening ceremonies. Haymitch asks whose idea the hand-holding was, and when Portia says it was Cinna's, he praises it as a "perfect touch of rebellion." He tells Katniss and Peeta to meet him for breakfast so he can tell them how to handle their first training session and sends them to bed

Peeta wants to know about the Avox, and—since it doesn't give any advantage—Katniss decides she can at least pay this debt to him. She's concerned about being overheard, so Peeta suggests the roof, which they are allowed to visit, protected from jumping off by an electrical field that throws back anything that goes over the edge. He takes her to a garden filled with wind chimes, where she whispers her story of being in the woods with Gale and seeing a boy and girl in tattered clothes, fleeing for their lives. Just as Gale and Katniss spotted them, a hovercraft appeared, dropping a net over the girl and shooting a spear through the boy, then hauling them up into the vessel and disappearing. She tells Peeta she doesn't know if the couple saw her, but she knows they did and feels guilty for failing to help them. Peeta and Katniss both suspect they were fleeing the Capitol, though Katniss can't understand why they'd do that or where they were going, since the only thing beyond District 12 is the ruins of District 13. Peeta blurts out, "I'd leave here," and then pretends he just wants to go home to avoid the Games, in case anyone's listening. Trying to get a fix on the relationship between Katniss and Gale, Peeta asks if Gale said goodbye to Katniss at the Justice Building, and Katniss says yes, adding the Peeta's father did, too. She is suspicious of Peeta's seemingly surprised expression. Peeta says his father knew Katniss's mother when they were young. In her room, Katniss finds the Avox she recognizes, and wants to apologize, but doesn't, even as she identifies a similarity between her watching the girl be captured with people watching the Hunger Games. Katniss is ashamed and wonders if the girl will enjoy watching her die.

36 *The Hunger Games: A Teaching Guide*

Strategy 12

Understanding Symbolism and Motifs

Directions: First, read the information. Then, answer the question or questions.

Symbolism is a technique in which a person, place, thing, or idea represents not only itself, but also a deeper, more complex reality beyond itself. There are universal symbols that are identifiable and used by people in many cultures and countries, like hearts to symbolize love. There are cultural symbols, the meaning of which is shared by people with the same ethnic background, faith, or other cultural connection, like the Christian cross or the Jewish Star of David. And there are national symbols, the meaning of which have meaning to a particular society, regardless of cultural group, station, or class a person comes from, like national flag of the United States, called the Stars and Stripes or Star-Spangled Banner.

When these types of symbols are used in a story, you must know something else outside of the story to interpret the symbol. Many cultural symbols come from religious works and mythology, whereas many national symbols arise from a particular nation's history and practices. For example, on the U.S. fla , the 13 stripes represent the 13 colonies, while the 50 stars represent the 50 states.

Another type of symbol is the contextual symbol, whose meaning applies only in the context of a particular work or works. For example, a mockingbird is neither a universal symbol, nor is it—in our country at least—a national symbol. In *To Kill a Mockingbird*, however, because the mockingbird is referred to in the title and throughout the work, it takes on a symbolic meaning. Repetition is often a key to identifying items that have a symbolic meaning.

Motif is the name used for a repeated thematic element of a story that often has a universal meaning. Folklorist Stith Thompson defined it as "the smallest element in a tale having a power to persist in tradition" (*The Folktale*, 1946, p. 415). Thompson defines three classes into which most motifs fall:

- the *actors* in a tale, including heroes, villains, and mentors
- *background elements*, including gifts and task-performing animals
- *single incidents*, including contests of strength and battles of wits

Wicked witches and sets of three tasks are two fairy tale motifs.

Motif analysis is most frequently applied to folktales and fairy tales, which are classified by the type, combination, and arrangement of motifs that they include, but a repeating element may be both a motif, if it is used in multiple works, and a symbol, if its use in a particular work is meant to call up things beyond its literal meaning. So be sure to follow up on any signs you see that symbolism and/or motifs are being used, no matter the genre.

1. Directions: Which of these items seem to you to be symbols and/or motifs in the portion of the book you've read so far? If you identify an item as a symbol, explain the symbolic meaning, insofar as you can identify it. If you identify it as a motif, list at least one other work it appears in. Continue to add to the chart as you read.

fire	Buttercup	Avoxes	cookies
the Hob	the woods	snares	coal
bread	the fence	rabbits	cosmetics
dandelions	mockingjay pin	the Hunger Games	

The Hunger Games: A Teaching Guide

Chapter 7

Training; Impressing the Gamemakers

Vocabulary

slumbers 86 sleeping
intertwines 86 connects with
gory 86 covered w/ blood
bolt 86 MM move suddenly and swiftly
emaciated 86 wasted away
probes 86 investigate by poking
arbitrarily 86 w/out reason or plan
deluged 86 flooded drenched
assent 87 agreement
smothered in 87 covered by
queasy 88 sick to one's stomach; nauseous
snares 89 devices w/ nooses to catch small game
assessment 89 evaluation
chuck 90 toss
glower 91 stare angrily
archery 91 the sport of shooting w/ a bow and arrows
underestimate 91 think too little of the the importance of
amiable 92 pleasant
stalk 92 MM to walk w/ strong, angry steps
demean 93 make appear less worthy
oblivious 93 unaware
obstacle course 93 race course w/ barriers
survival skills 93 knowledge and techniques that help people in difficult situations stay alive using tools and nature
combative 93 fightin
exertion 94 work
technically 94 going by the rules (implies that the rules are often violated)
contempt 94 scorn

project 95 convey
arrogance 95 offensive display of feeling superior to others
brutality 95 great cruelty
sober 95 serious
intimidate 95 inspire fear by a display of force or power
incompetent 95 unskilled; inadequate
camouflage 95 act of concealing by altering the appearance of something
preoccupied 95 having one's mind already focused on something when something else happens
inaccessible 96 beyond reach
break in 96 interrupt
mediocre 96 unsatisfactory; less capable
fixated 97 focused completely
rowdily 97 in a rough disorderly way
animate 98 make lively
right on cue 98 at exactly the right time
stature 98 height
grill 99 question closely
sanity 99 good sense; balance
surly 99 bad-tempered; rude; like an enemy
slated 100 scheduled
linger 100 stay
flawless 101 perfect
quiver 101 MM a case to hold arrows
silhouettes 101 black outlines, filled in w/ black
skewer 101 pierce through and through
sever 101 cut through, dividing in two
upstaged 101 overshadowed

Journal and Discussion Questions

1. If you were asked to interpret Katniss's shower as symbolic, what would you say?
2. Categorize Chapters 1–7 by the day(s) of the story on which they take place.
3. Explain what you understand to be the reasons behind Haymitch's training advice.
4. Consider whether the evidence in this chapter would support the conclusion that Mrs. Mellark knew that Peeta burnt the bread on purpose. Share your thoughts.
5. Do you find it believable that Katniss thinks eeta is insulting her by saying she'll win sponsors? Explain your response.
6. What effect does Katniss have that Peeta says she is unaware of?
7. Why do you think the Gamemakers are keeping an eye on District 12?
8. Which skills do Katniss and Peeta excel in, despite their efforts to appear mediocre?
9. What motivation might Rue have for shadowing the District 12 tributes in training?
10. Do you think Katniss and Peeta view their relationship in the same way? Provide evidence to support your view.
11. What do you think the Gamemakers will make of Katniss's performance?
12. Summarize the chapter by comparing and contrasting the three days of training.

Summary

At breakfast on the first day of training, Katniss sees that she and Peeta have been given matching outfit , which irritates her. She is tempted to point out that this "twin thing" can't last, given the nature of the Games, but remembers that Haymitch told her to obey her stylist.

Katniss and Peeta agree to be coached together, and Haymitch asks them to tell him what skills they have. Peeta says he has none. Katniss says she can hunt with a bow and arrow, but undersells her talent when Haymitch asks if she's good. This leads Peeta to speak for her excellence, based on the game she sells his father. Katniss is suspicious of why he'd praise her and in retaliation, points out Peeta's strength and wrestling skills to Haymitch, declaring that if he gets a knife, he'll have a chance in hand-to-hand combat, whereas she'd be in trouble. Peeta retorts that she'll be up a tree picking off people with arrows. He reveals that his mother, in saying good-bye, observed that maybe District 12 would finally have a winner, meaning Katniss, saying, "She's a survivor," and Katniss retorts that she's only a survivor because someone (Peeta) helped her. Peeta says that she'll get sponsors for the arena, and when Katniss says he will, too, he turns to Haymitch and says, "She has no idea. The effect she can have." Katniss doesn't know what he means, but assumes it is an insult.

Haymitch advises Katniss and Peeta to avoid their strong suits during the three days of training, only revealing them in their private session with the Gamemakers at the end. He adds that they are to stay together all the time in public, and when they both object, he insists that they not only be together, but appear pleasant. After stalking off to her room to be alone until its time to go to training, Katniss begins to wonder if the 'insult' from Peeta is actually a compliment.

Arriving at the training session with Peeta, Katniss discovers that they are the only two dressed alike. They are told that combat between tributes is prohibited, and while the training stations are being listed, Katniss observes that all the boys and half the girls are bigger than she is. She had only really expected big, strong tributes to come from Districts 1, 2, and 4, where—although its technically illegal to train before the reaping—tributes are trained throughout their lives. Although they follow Haymitch's directions, Peeta can't help excelling in hand-to-hand combat, and Katniss in identifying edible plants, as the Gamemakers sit in elevated stands and watch. The tributes have lunch in the Training Center, during which Peeta shows Katniss the unique bread type from each district. After each day of training, Katniss and Peeta debrief with Haymitch and Effie before bed. On the second day, they notice that Rue, the girl from District 11 is shadowing them and has some of the same skills as Katniss. As they head to their rooms on the second night, Peeta makes a joke, and rather than respond, Katniss suggests that they don't have to keep being pleasant to each other when no one's looking. Peeta agrees, but Katniss notes that his voice sounds tired.

On the third day of training, each tribute gets to show off to the Gamemakers, in order of district—first the boy tribute, then the girl. When Katniss's turn comes, she sees that the Gamemakers are bored. She picks up a bow, and although it takes her some practice to get used to it, she hits a dummy through the heart, severs the rope that holds the boxing sand bag, and shoots a hanging light high above, creating a shower of sparks. But the Gamemakers are mostly ignoring her, more interested in the roast pig that has just been served to them. Furious, Katniss shoots the apple out of the pig's mouth, shocking the Gamemakers, and rather than wait for dismissal, walks out.

Chapter 7, cont.

The Hunger Games: A Teaching Guide

Chapter 8

The Scoring; How Katniss and Gale Met

Vocabulary

gaping 103 staring w/ open mouths
bolt 103 MM fasten w/ a bolt; lock
leniency 104 tolerance of low standards
sic 104 send an attack
irredeemably 104 w/out possibility of returning to good standing
unattainably 104 unable to be reached
splotchy 105 covered w/ big irregular spots
chitchat 105 unimportant conversation
provoked 106 targeted by behavior that angers and stirs to action
ticks off 106 makes angry
defiantly 106 in a way meant to challenge authority
dunks 107 sticks something into liquid
guffaws 107 laughs loudly, w/out restraint
impressive 108 able to arouse admiration
burrow 109 dig oneself deep into

drift off 109 fall asleep
reprieved 109 forgiven
arduous 109 difficult requiring great labor
pungent 109 w/ a sharp, penetrating smell
quest 109 search
afoot 110 stirring (and visible)
lugging 110 dragging w/ great effort
materialize 110 appear suddenly, as if from nothing
audible 110 able to be heard
transformed 111 completely changed
menacing 111 threatening
grudgingly 111 unwillingly
confidant 112 one to whom one tells secrets
pang 112 sudden, brief, sensation, often of pain or longing
motives 112 reasons for doing something

Journal and Discussion Questions

1. Katniss aimed at and hit an apple. Why would say she shot at the Gamemakers?
2. Compare and contrast how Peeta and Gale helped Katniss get food.
3. List as many motivations as you can for Peeta asking to be coached separately.
4. Make a line graph of Katniss's emotional state through the chapter. Label it.

Summary

Katniss heads to District 12's quarters, throwing the bow and quiver aside and avoiding tears until she reaches her room and bolts the door. Fearful that she will be arrested, executed, or turned into an Avox—or worse, that her family will be targeted—she thinks of what she might have done differently. Haymitch and Effie come to her door, but she shouts at them to go away and cries for an hour before she finally calms down Realizing that they still need District 12 to have a girl tribute, she figures that any punishment will either come in the arena or in a score so low that no one will sponsor her.

At dinner, she finds the stylists have joined the group. After they eat, Haymitch asks how bad the scoring sessions were. Peeta answers immediately, saying that they didn't bother to watch him. Katniss explains that she shot an apple out of a pig's mouth right by the Gamekeepers. Cinna asks cautiously how they responded, and Katniss admits that she doesn't know because she walked out. Recalling her promise to Prim, she feels terrible, but is somewhat relieved when Haymitch says he doesn't think she'll be arrested or that her family will be punished. The fact that he thinks she only has to look forward to a hell of a time in the arena—which she expected anyway—cheers her up, and she is even more cheered when he gets her to tell how they responded, and she recalls one man falling into the punch bowl, which draws general laughter. Portia adds that scores only matter if they're good because talented tributes sometimes strategically hide their capabilities to get a low score. After dinner, they watch the televised announcement of the scores. Peeta gets an eight, and Katniss gets an 11—the top training score, and Haymitch points out that having a temper mightn't seem bad to the Gamemakers, who have to put on a show.

Watching the sunrise the next morning, a Sunday, Katniss thinks about what the day would be like at home, and this recalls to mind her first meeting with Gale in the woods in October of the year of her father's death. On her way home from hunting, she spotted twitch-up snares above her head, and since she'd had no success with snares, she was stopping to examine them, when a voice warned her of danger. It was Gale, 14 at the time. He misunderstood her name as "Catnip" because she said it so softly, and that became his nickname for her. He was as interested in her bow as she was in his snares, and they agreed to trade a bow for learning to set snares. The acquaintance grew into a partnership as Gale became her confidant and there are hints that it could become more. Katniss contrasts her trust in Gale with her suspicions of Peeta. Effie calls her to breakfast, where Haymitch informs her that Peeta has asked to be coached separately.

Strategy 13

Understanding Character Traits as Ranges

Directions: First, read the information. Then, answer the question or questions.

We often speak of **character traits** as absolutes—that is, characters either have them or not. So we might describe a character as greedy and obnoxious. This is useful for a start. But even a character that we recognize as greedy and obnoxious in general can be more or less greedy and more or less obnoxious, depending on the situation. Considering character traits as ranges, rather than absolutes, can be the first step in taking a more realistic view of the complex thing we call character, particularly in longer works of fiction and help us to interpret apparent inconsistencies in a fruitful way.

To this end, let's consider character traits as existing on a continuum, a scale with opposite traits at the ends and a whole range of possible points in between. For example:

charming————————————————————————surly

Think about Katniss: she's often a surly, unfriendly person. In the first anecdote she tells about herself, she tries to drown Buttercup, who still keeps her at arm's length. Now think about the staged conversations in Chapter 7. It seems that Katniss can be charming as well. You can see that to say that Katniss is or isn't surly would not come near to telling the whole story.

1. For each continuum, collect information as you read for each of the characters listed below it. When you are done reading, write a paragraph telling how each character moves along the continuum during the course of the book.

    honest————————————————————————deceptive
    (Katniss, Peeta, the Gamemakers)

    self-serving————————————————————————generous
    (Katniss, Peeta, Haymitch)

    insightful————————————————————————misguided
    (Katniss, Haymitch, Peeta, Rue, Gale)

    responsible————————————————————————irresponsible
    (Katniss, Peeta, Haymitch)

2. Choose a single character and write a full-page description of her or his character traits. Explain how his or her behavior varies along each continuum that you identify. Use the information you have acquired so far, and add to your description as you finish the book

3. Write a paragraph about Katniss's development as a partner to others. Explain how this development relates to the development of various character traits.

The Hunger Games: A Teaching Guide 41

Chapter 9 — The Interviews

Vocabulary

ludicrous 114 absurd; ridiculous
pretense 114 an act of pretending
wobbling 115 moving unsteadily side to side
swoops down 115 moves in suddenly
posture 115 body position; how one carries oneself
gestures 115 motions that express or add to one's words
banal 115 ordinary, boring, and not original
aggravating 115 annoying
aloof 116 choosing to remain at a distance
intrigued 116 deeply interested
eccentric 116 different from the norm
self-deprecating 116 modest
sullen 116 maintaining a gloomy silence
hostile 116 acting like an enemy
counter 117 retort
ferocity 118 savage fierceness
despise 118 feel contempt for or disgust w/
reproachful 118 full of blame
radiant 121 brilliant
stage fright 123 pre-performance nerves

pulse 124 throbbing of arteries caused by contractions of the heart
temples 124 flattened areas on each side of the forehead
virtually 124 almost entirely
longevity 125 long life
freakish 125 bizarre; abnormal
provocative 125 seductive
elusive 125 unable to be pinned down
absorbent 126 able to take in moisture
gossamer 126 very thin, light, fine fabric
a hush falls 126 it gets quiet
tremulous 126 shaky
banter 126 playful conversation
confidentially 127 as if speaking in private
protective 128 intended to protect
hooting 128 shouting a loud owl-like cry
rigidity 129 inability to move
subtle 129 barely noticeable
get-go 130 beginning
unconvincing 130 not believable
unrequited 130 not returned
mystified 130 puzzled

Journal and Discussion Questions

1. What detail(s) from Chapter 8 would support the feeling of betrayal that Katniss admits to in Chapter 9?
2. Do you agree with Katniss's assessment of Peeta's decision to be coached alone?
3. How does Effie Trinket put her foot in her mouth when coaching Katniss for the interview?
4. How does the choice of cooperating with Effie's and Haymitch's coaching efforts appear to Katniss? How does it look to Haymitch?
5. In what way does Mr. Everdeen's joke about the plant she's named after resonate with Katniss's experience in trying to prepare for the interview?
6. What did you infer from the juxtaposition of the scene with Haymitch and the scene with the Avox?
7. Katniss seems not to remember Haymitch's first words about her in Chapter 2 when considering Cinna's statement that she has spirit. Do you think the Cinna and Haymitch see similar things in Katniss or not? Explain your response.
8. How has Katniss's attitude changed from her sessions with Effie and Haymitch to her discussion of approach with Cinna?
9. Do you agree with Katniss that Haymitch is destructive? Explain your answer.
10. Before reading the end of the chapter, why did you think Haymitch wanted Peeta and Katniss to still act like a couple? What did you think when the chapter was complete?
11. What do you imagine Caesar Flickerman thinks of his job?
12. How do you appraise Peeta's interview? Tell the reasons behind your judgment.
13. Write two summaries of the chapter, one in which Peeta is being honest and another in which he is being strategic. In each case, discuss his motivation and what he hopes to gain through his actions.

Summary

Katniss feels unaccountably betrayed by the coaching change, and while being a tribute in the Games doesn't allow for trust, some part of her did trust Peeta based on history. Thinking it over, she is relieved that they can stop pretending to be friends.

Haymitch tells her that she will have four hours each of interview presentation training with Effie and content training with him

Katniss's time with Effie is spent learning to walk in a full-length gown wearing high heels and speaking with a smile, while making eye contact and gesturing. Katniss finds it repugnant to be asked to smile at people who are betting on how long she'll live.

Haymitch tries to figure out an approach for Katniss, pointing out that although her volunteering for her sister, Cinna's fire costume, and her score have gotten peoples' attention, they don't actually know her. Katniss asks about Peeta's approach, which Haymitch describes as likable and self-deprecating; in contrast, he describes Katniss's normal style as "sullen and hostile," which offends her. Haymitch urges her to delight him as they role play the interview, with Haymitch asking questions and Katniss answering, but Katniss is so angry with Haymitch and finds the whole thing so unjust and invasive, that it doesn't work. Haymitch points out that sharing information about herself is key to attracting sponsors, but Katniss responds that they are taking her future, and she won't give them her past. Given that, Haymitch suggests that she lie, but she says she's no good at it. He makes other suggestions, but nothing works, and he starts drinking. Finally, he says he gives up and suggests she try to disguise how much she despises the audience.

Katniss has dinner in her room, eats herself sick, and smashes the dishes. The Avox whom she recognized comes in to turn down her bed, and Katniss sends her away, but she doesn't go. Instead, she gently wipes Katniss's face and her bloody hands where she has been cut by a plate with a damp cloth. Katniss confesses that she should have saved her, but the Avox indicates that Katniss would have become an Avox, too, had she tried. They clean the room together, and then the Avox turns down her bed, tucks Katniss in, and leaves.

In the morning, Katniss's prep team prepares her for the interview—the last event before the Games begin the following day. When they have finished Cinna brings in her dress, which looks like tongues of flam , especially when she twirls. She confesses her unpreparedness for the interview to Cinna, who speaks about her spirit—an idea that captures her imagination. Cinna suggests that instead of speaking to the audience at large, she find him on the platform and speak to him, answering honestly. He reminds her that the audience loves her already. Just before the tributes go onstage, Haymitch surprises her by reminding her and Peeta to act like a happy couple.

The interviewer, Caesar Flickerman, has a Capitol resident's love of cosmetic alteration, but, says Katniss, does his best to present each tribute in a positive light. Katniss watches the other districts' tributes be interviewed, girl first then boy. When it is her turn, she is able to find Cinna, give honest answers, and please the audience, while twirling in her dress draws great admiration. Peeta talks easily with Caesar, even joking. At the end of the interview, Caesar asks him about a special girl, and he says he's had a crush on a girl forever, but she didn't realize he was alive until the reaping. Caesar suggests that he win and go home to claim her, but Peeta says that winning won't help him. When Caesar, mystified asks why, Peeta explains that the girl came to the Games with him.

Chapter 9, cont.

Strategy 14

Identifying References, Allusions, and Parody

Directions: First, read the information. Then, answer the question or questions.

A **reference** is an explicit mention of something outside the work you are currently reading. It could be a reference to a real or imaginary event, person, or place; to another literary work (often in a quotation); to an aspect of culture; or to a fact. References are often documented.

An **allusion** is an indirect reference—one that you need to recognize as a reference without the author telling you that it is one. After you recognize the allusion, you need to figure out what it means in context. Note that an allusion is a reference to something specifi , and this is how it differs from a motif, which is a universal or work-specifi , repeated element. For example, in the sentence—

> Going into the woods to poach game to share with the hungry can get you in trouble, whether you wear a hood or a dress of flame ,

—the word *hood* is an allusion to a specific outlaw, Robin of Locksley (called *Robin Hood*), while the words *dress of flames* are an allusion to another specific character, Katniss Everdeen. But *stealing from the rich to give to the poor* is a motif that occurs in multiple works of art (view a list at http://tvtropes.org/pmwiki/pmwiki.php/Main/JustLikeRobinHood).

Many allusions are to references that support or reinforce the meaning in the text. For example, the name of *Panem*, the Latin names of the Capitol residents, and the use of gladiatorial games are all allusions to ancient Rome and work to build a unified idea of the society in which Katniss lives. Checking out any Latin and Greek names in fiction may prove valuable.

But this is not the only possible purpose of an allusion. **Parody** is a special type of allusion that recalls to mind something in order to make fun of it (or just create humor) through imitation coupled with other devices such as exaggeration and contrast. A parody of an event or work of art may focus on the overarching plot or the stylistic peculiarities and propensities of the original and call attention to them. When style is being parodied, stylistic idiosyncrasies are made obvious, often by overuse. When the original work is pompous, offensive, overly serious or sentimental, makes much of something trivial, or is just plain obtuse, parody can function as criticism as well as humor.

It is important that a parody be similar enough to the original that the audience can recognize what is being parodied. A parody of a story, for example, might keep the subject or plot and some of the wording, but change the characters, like the recent treatments of the classics to which zombies have been added. Collins's parody of reality television keeps an aspect of the premise (live interviews of "real" people—not actors) and creates a scenario in which the context (to decide whom to bet on as a group of children fight to the death) is so disturbing that the net effect is a combination of disgust and horror.

A **caricature** is a particular type of parody—one that is exaggerated and often uncomplimentary and oversimplified Collins's parody of the genre of reality television is far from complimentary and can be called *caricature*. Caricature can also focus on a well-known individual.

1. As you read the rest of the book, note elements of reality television that Collins is parodying.

Test: Chapters 1–9

Vocabulary

Look at each group of words. Tell why it is important in the story.

1. savages, barbarism
2. poaching, game, prey, spoils
3. podium, intones, protocol
4. laughingstock, plummets, spunk, unconscious
5. mockingjay, muttations, jabberjay
6. skewer, severed, upstaged, gaping
7. radiant, gossamer, unrequited

Essay Topics

1. In Chapter 4, Katniss makes two striking observations that involve nature: on p. 49, she mentions how kind people "root" inside her; on p. 51, she characterizes the woods as her family's "savior." What conclusions can you draw from this?

2. The odds, as Katniss has said, are not in her favor. But there are some things in her favor. Assess what Katniss has going for her.

3. What do you think of Collins's choice to have Katniss say that the other district's tributes don't "hold a candle" to District 12?

4. Do you find Katniss's criticisms of the Capitol and its inhabitants—explicit and implied—valid? Explain why you think as you do.

5. If you were the author of this story, what would happen next? Explain how you would develop the plot.

6. What effect do you think Peeta's declaration of love will have on Katniss? What leads you to this conclusion?

7. On p. 4, Katniss puts on her boots before she puts on her trousers. Anyone who's tried to pull on pants over shoes may wonder at this. Why do you think Collins had Katniss dress in this order?

8. On p. 62, Katniss discusses how her prep team are "so unlike people" and compares them to birds. Is this different than Flavius saying to Katniss, "You almost look like a human being now"? Explain your thinking.

9. Do you think that by talking to Cinna during the interview, Katniss actually avoided behaving like a "trained dog" (p. 117)? Explain your answer.

The Hunger Games: A Teaching Guide 45

Chapter 10

PART II "THE GAMES"
"An Object of Love"; "To Die as Myself"

Vocabulary

downcast 133 looking down
deafening 133 so loud that nothing else can be heard
breached 134 crossed
veer 134 change direction suddenly
entourages 134 people who travel w/ one
shards 134 sharp slivers of pottery or glass
aghast 134 overcome w/ shock and awe
star-crossed 135 ill-fated
bluff 136 something misleading
waft 137 floa
privilege 138 honor
fatigue 139 tiredness
terrain 139 landscape
frigid 139 ice cold
concealment 140 hiding
barren 140 lacking plant life
liven up 140 add excitement to
eludes 140 escapes from
commotion 140 noise
disgrace 141 cause shame/embarrassment
inferior 142 of comparatively less value
ruminating 142 pondering; wondering
offense 142 insult
mocking 142 showing scorn
patronizing 142 acting as if someone is inferior to oneself
endearment 142 term showing warm affection
cannibalism 143 eating of human flesh by another human
speculation 143 guessing
avalanche 143 sudden descent of a mass of ice, snow, rocks or soil from high up
catacombs 143 Literally, "underground chambers"
syringe 143 device for injecting material under the skin
whereabouts 144 location
delectable 144 delicious
reenactments 145 recreating past events by acting them out
tawny 145 dark yellowish-brown color
obsessively 146 continually, w/out being able to stop
conscious 147 aware

Journal and Discussion Questions

1. Katniss attributes real pain to Caesar (p. 133). Explain why you do or don't agree with her assessment.
2. When Katniss says she knows better (p. 134), what does she mean?
3. How do you imagine Haymitch helped Peeta with his idea for the interview?
4. The term "star-crossed" is an allusion. Identify the source. What does it mean in the context of *The Hunger Games*?
5. Do you think Katniss is right that she should have been told of Peeta's plan? If not, what is your take on the situation?
6. Why does Peeta say his performance was a bluff?
7. How can the tributes wield influence outside the arena during the Games
8. What does Effie's goodbye to Katniss and Peeta reveal about her?
9. What does the fact that Katniss keeps her nail polish as a remembrance of who she is to the audience say to you?
10. Collins uses the word *silhouette* of Peeta sitting in the shadows on the roof the night before the Games. She also used it on page 101. How does the first usage inform the second?
11. Peeta says he wants to die as himself. In your own words, tell what you believe he means.
12. Are there any options for opting out of the Games? Explain your answer.
13. What conclusions do you draw about the Games from the anecdote about Titus?
14. The term *catacombs* is another allusion. Identify the original meaning. What does it mean in the context of *The Hunger Games*?
15. The Capitol uses the agricultural term *reaping* to refer to the choosing of tributes for a fight to the death They use the term *Launch Room* for the room from which each tribute enters the arena. What do you make of these uses of language? What do you make of the fact that in the districts, the Launch Room is called the *Stockyards*?
16. Given what you know of the Capitol, do you find it believable that the review board would pass Katniss's mockingjay pin? Explain your answer.

17. What one thing does Katniss find "hopeful" when she enters the arena? Why would this seem hopeful to her?
18. Summarize the chapter from Cinna's point of view.

Summary

Katniss doesn't immediately realize that Peeta means her. Caesar sympathizes with Peeta and assures him that he can't be blamed for his feelings, clarifying for the audience that this is the first Katniss has heard of it and telling Peeta that the hearts of Panem are with him. Katniss notes that the screens show shots of her and Peeta standing close but separate—never to be joined—bespeaking their tragedy. But, she adds, she knows better. Back in their quarters, Katniss slams into Peeta, knocking him into an urn so that he falls among the shards, cutting his hands. He's shocked, and she says he had no right to speak about her the way he did. Learning what happened, Haymitch calls her a fool, saying Peeta gave her something she couldn't acquire herself: he has made her seem desirable, so that now everyone is talking about the "star-crossed lovers from District 12." Katniss objects that it's not true, and Haymitch says it's all a show, and he can use it to get sponsors. Cinna seconds Haymitch, but Katniss insists she should have been told. Peeta implicitly defends her, saying she's worried about Gale's view, but that Gale's sure to see that Peeta was bluffing, and besides, Katniss didn't say she loved him. Katniss realizes that her interview lacked substance, while Peeta has made her an object of love. Katniss finally apologizes, and Haymitch herds the group to the dinner table. Peeta has to leave to get his hands bandaged, and Katniss feels guilty that he will start the Games on the following day with injuries. Watching the replays after dinner confirms that Katniss was silly and giggly, while Peeta was charming and made her more desirable to potential sponsors.

Effie and Haymitch say goodbye: only the stylists accompany the tributes to the stadium. Haymitch's final advice is to flee the launch site as soon as the starting gong sounds. The Cornucopia of supplies at the launch site is always the site of a blood bath, and they should get far away and seek water.

Katniss showers off her interview makeup, but keeps the flames that have been painted on her fingernails as a reminder of who she is to the audience. Realizing that she can't sleep, she goes up to the roof, where she finds Peeta. She apologizes again for hurting his hands, but Peeta deflects her concern, saying he's never been a contender. Katniss rejects this, but Peeta says its true and that he wants to die as himself, not be turned into a monster. Katniss asks if this means he won't kill anyone, and Peeta says he's sure he will when he has to but he doesn't want to allow himself to be owned and be only a piece in the Capitol's Games. Katniss says that that's how it works and asks who cares. Peeta says he does, and asks what else he could care about at this point. Katniss tells him to remember Haymitch's advice and care about staying alive. He gives her an mocking answer, calling her "sweetheart," as Haymitch does, which angers her. She retorts that he can spend his last hours planning a noble death; she hopes to spend her last hours in District 12. He says he wouldn't be surprised if she did and asks her to greet his mother for him. She tells him she will and walks away.

In the morning, Cinna comes to guide Katniss to the roof, where a hovercraft appears. As soon as she is inside, a tracker is installed in her arm. They are dropped off at the arena and taken to Katniss's Launch Room. Cinna helps Katniss dress and fastens her mockingjay pin to her shirt. When the announcement comes, she walks to the metal launch plate, as Cinna repeats Haymitch's advice, and tells her he'd bet on her if he were allowed to. They hold hands until the glass cylinder lowered over her breaks their hold, and he signals her to hold her chin up. When the metal plates of all the tributes have risen into the arena, the announcer of the Hunger Games, Claudius Templesmith, speaks the words that start the Games.

Chapter 10, cont.

Chapter 11

The Games Begin; Search for Water; Peeta Joins Careers

Vocabulary

equidistant 148 the same distance
strewn 148 scattered randomly
sparse 148 thinly spread; opposite of dense
bounty 149 many items, supplied at no cost
salvation 149 life-saver
repulsed 150 repelled; disgusted
adrenaline 151 hormone that increases heart rate and blood pressure in response to anger or fear
reflexively 151 w/out thought
pursue 151 follow
hacking 151 MM chopping w/ sharp blades and heavy, irregular blows
void 151 an empty and unknown space
serrated 151 w/ a notched cutting edge
botched 151 ruined
rejuvenating 152 restoring; uplifting
illusion 152 deceptive or false impression
trekking 152 traveling slowly
casualties 152 losses through death
dispersed 152 spread out

fatalities 152 deaths
conjure up 153 imagine
directive 153 order
arbitrary 153 random
dehydration 154 serious lack of water
provisions 154 supplies
iodine 154 antiseptic used to purify water
muffles 154 lessens the noise of
stalking 155 MM pursuing as prey
priority 155 top consideration
abundance 155 generous amount
precaution 156 safety measure
radiating 156 reflecting heat ba k
invaluable 156 priceless
conflicting 157 contrary; opposite
gratitude 157 thankfulness
scuffling 158 irregular sounds
foul 158 offensive; filthy
devising 159 planning
alliances 159 teams
brutish 160 like an animal; brutal

Journal and Discussion Questions

1. Discuss imagined reactions from Districts 2, 9, 12, and the Capitol to Katniss's first encounter in the arena How does this serve the Capitol?
2. Was Katniss wise to bypass Haymitch's advice? Explain your thinking.
3. What does Katniss's reaction to the fire-lighting tribute s behavior show?
4. Summarize the chapter from Peeta's point of view. Provide at least two alternative scenarios, depending on why he has allied himself with the Careers.

Summary

Standing on her circle, Katniss notes the life-giving supplies near the Cornucopia, the piney woods to her left and back, and a lake to her right, while a steep slope ahead hides the view. She spots a silver bow and arrows, and determines to abandon Haymitch's advice and grab them. But Peeta seems to be shaking his head just as the gong sounds, and hesitating, she loses her opportunity. Angrily, she grabs a sheet of plastic right in front of her and fights over an orange backpack with a boy who is knifed by another tribute. A second knife, thrown at her as she flee , lodges in the backpack, and she retrieves it as she heads into the woods and begins searching for water, wondering if Peeta is already dead. When she is exhausted, she stops and examines her backpack, realizing that she will need to camouflage it. It contains a reflective sleeping bag, a pack each of crackers and beef jerky, a small coil of wire, matches, a bottle of iodine, a pair of sunglasses, and an empty half-gallon plastic bottle. Worried that the lake may be the only water, she remembers seeing a rabbit, and reasons that it must have a place to drink. She keeps moving, eating pine bark scrapings to stave off hunger and save the food. As it gets late, she sets two twitch-up snares with the wire and climbs a willow with a sturdy fork, arranging herself and her backpack in the sleeping bag and belting herself to the tree. As it grows cold, she decides that getting the backpack was the right choice.

When night falls, the anthem signals the beginning of the death recap, shown each night on screens above the arena. It reveals that Peeta is among the 13 tributes still alive. Katniss feels very confused about Peeta—grateful for the edge provided by his professed love, angry at his superior stance on the roof, and terrified of coming face-to-face with him in the arena. She falls asleep but is awakened by snapping, which she eventually identifies as someone building a fire several hundred yards from her. She is furious because she knows the fire will attract other tributes who are out hunting, and it does. As the attack on the fire starter commences, Katniss realizes that the Career Tributes are fighting in a pack. When they move away, as required, to let a hovercraft collect the body, they end up only about 10 yards from the tree Katniss is in, but are puzzled because the cannon announcing a death has not fired One of the group suggests that maybe the girl isn't dead. When another tribute says he'll go back and finish her off, and Katniss recognizes Peeta's voice, she is so shocked that she almost falls out of the tree.

48   *The Hunger Games: A Teaching Guide*

Strategy 15   Reading Dialogue

Directions: First, read the information. Then, answer the question or questions.

Dialogue is the name for conversation that takes place in narrative. Even one person speaking is characteristically referred to as *dialogue*, even though normally *dialogue* refers to a conversation involving two or more people. Dialogue is distinguished from narration and description.

Sometimes dialogue is attributed with dialogue tags like "says Gale." When more than two people are involved, and there aren't dialogue tags, you should decide whether it's important to know who said what to help you decide how closely to read. For example, when the Career pack debates why they haven't heard a cannon yet, their dialogue is not attributed, and this is a sign from Collins that identifying the exact speaker for each lines is not important. Nevertheless, repeat speakers can be identified from the content of what is said. When knowing who is speaking *is* important and can't be understood from content, look for the following signs:

- **Alternating dialogue**. Dialogue between two people goes back and forth, by nature. It is an exchange of ideas, views, thoughts, and the like. So every *other* line (1, 3, 5, 7, 9 or 2, 4, 6, 8, 10, if they were numbered) is spoken by the same character.

- **Vocatives**. A *vocative* is a word that shows who is being addressed in a sentence. When—during the debate about Peeta's interview—Cinna says, "He's right, Katniss," (p. 136), he leaves no doubt about whom he is addressing. Almost always, the next person to speak after a sentence with a vocative is the person addressed.

- **Speech characteristics**. Just as people have certain habits of movement, they have certain habits of speech—characteristic expressions that can help you to recognize them, even when you have very little else to help you recognize who is talking. This is called *idiolect*, which simply means "an individual's speech."

WHAT ISN'T SAID

In the dialogue of *The Hunger Games*, sometimes one character interrupts another or a character interrupts himself. And sometimes a character chooses not to complete a thought. Pay attention to the unsaid in dialogue. Try to imagine what the speaker had intended to say.

LANGUAGE SHIFTS

People speak differently in different settings—they adapt their speech to the people and social context. Effie Trinket is notorious for failing to do this. As you read any book, watch for the ways in which people vary and do not vary their language to meet the social situation.

1. When Katniss meets her mother and sister in the Justice Building, after Prim asks Katniss to promise she'll try to win, someone says that if Katniss won, the family would be as rich as Haymitch (p. 36). Who says this? How do you know?

2. There is a series of unattributed comments after the attack on the fire-lighting tribute (. 160). Identify which lines belong to the same tribute and explain the strategies you used to figure it out

3. Identify the speakers of these phrases and how these phrases differ from other dialogue in the book: "I was still in bed!" "I had just had my eyebrows dyed!" "I swear I nearly fainted!"

The Hunger Games: A Teaching Guide   49

Writer's Forum 3 — Writing Dialogue

Writer's Forum

Directions: First, read the information. Then, answer the question or questions.

Dialogue is a particularly powerful way to reveal a character's thoughts, personality, tastes, and culture. The language that each character uses can reflect such important characteristics as age, education, and background. The level of formality the character uses can reflect his or her personality and approach to life as well as the social situation in which the speech takes place. Dialogue can also reveal relationships. How two (or more) people speak to each other shows a lot about their feelings for each other. Do they give each other a turn to speak? What tones of voice do they use? Do they use polite phrases or insults? Do they make each other laugh?

In terms of text organization, dialogue can help to break up narrative passages and can be more interesting than paraphrased speech.

Rules for Writing Dialogue

A. Start a new paragraph each time you switch speakers, or if a speaker speaking for a long time switches topics.

B. Punctuate dialogue to clearly show which words are the exact words that each speaker says. Follow these rules:

- **For tags before the speaker's words**:
1. Begin the tag with a capital letter.
2. Follow the tag with a comma, a space, and an opening quotation mark.
3. Begin the quotation of the sentence with a capital letter.
4. End the quotation of the sentence with the proper punctuation (./?/!)
5. Close the quotation marks.

- **For tags in between the speaker's words:**
1. Begin with opening quotation marks, followed by a capital letter.
2. Follow the first part of the quotation with a comma if it is in the middle of a sentence or if it is the end of a sentence that would normally end with a period (or ?/! if it is the end of an interrogative or exclamatory sentence), end quotation marks, and a space.
3. Write the tag and follow it with a comma, a space, and opening quotation marks.
4. Finish a sentence by beginning with a lowercase letter (unless it's a proper noun); start a new sentence with a capital letter. End either with the proper punctuation (./?/!)
5. Close the quotation marks.

- **For tag after the speaker's words:**
1. Begin with opening quotation marks and start the quotation with a capital letter.
2. If the quotation would normally end with a period, substitute a comma. If it would normally end with a ? or !, use the ? or !
3. Follow the end punctuation with closing quotation marks and a space.
4. Add the tag.
5. End the sentence with the appropriate punctuation, usually a period.

1. While watching the broadcast of the first d y of the Hunger Games Effie and H ymitch likely had a few very opinionated things to say. Write a dialogue for them.

50 *The Hunger Games: A Teaching Guide*

Chapter 12

Finding Water; the Wall of Fire

Chapter 12 Page 161

Vocabulary

foresight 161 planning
rustling 161 soft sounds like leaves rubbing together
gait 161 walking
lapdogs 161 favorites of those in power
gall 162 shameless boldness; impudence
sappy 162 sentimental
puke 162 throw up
hoist 163 lift
digesting 163 considering; taking in
perplexed 164 puzzled
foliage 164 leaves
imprudent 164 unwise
innards 164 internal parts of the body
charred 164 burnt till it's blackened

quench 165 lessen
dissecting 165 analyzing
canopy 165 treetops
tactic 166 approach; way of doing things
unrelenting 166 unchanging
scarcity 167 short supply
gingerly 167 gently and cautiously
forthcoming 168 provided; arriving
deluded 168 deceived; misled
accountable 168 responsible
searing 169 scorching; burning
signifying 170 being a sign or indication of
abstain 170 hold back by voluntary effort
purifying 170 making pure and safe
bewilderment 171 confusion

Journal and Discussion Questions

1. Katniss has an explanation for Peeta's injuries and why he hasn't yet told the Careers how she scored the 11. Give alternative explanations for both.
2. How does Katniss plan to make the most of her expected camera time?
3. Based on the information in this chapter, what do you think would have happened if Katniss had done exactly what Haymitch told her to do?
4. Summarize the chapter from what you imagine is Haymitch's point of view, watching the broadcast.

Summary

Saved from falling to the ground by the belt, Katniss is hanging below the branch, with her feet braced on the tree trunk. A Career encourages Peeta to check on the "dead" tribute, and as he goes, Katniss sees his bruised face and a bloody bandage on his arm, and hears his limp. She concludes that, despite warning her away, he got involved in the fight for supplies, and figures she can handle that contradiction, but doesn't know how to accept his teaming up with the Careers. She concludes that his talk of nobility on the roof was just another mind game. With Peeta is out of earshot, the Careers point out that he's their best chance of finding Katniss, and Katniss learns both that they think she was taken in by the romance story and that Peeta has not yet told them how she got the 11—perhaps, she reasons, saving this information so they'll keep him alive.

After they leave but before getting down, Katniss plans how she wants to appear for the first camera that can capture her expression, and when she comes out from the leaves, gives a knowing smile. Checking her snares before departing the area, she finds a rabbit, which she cleans, guts, and cooks on the fire of the unfortunate dead tribute. As she walks in the opposite direction to the tribute pack and eats, she is careful to hide her emotions, while she ponders whether Peeta joining up with the Careers has doomed the romance story and, therefore, the hope of sponsors. She thinks that maybe they can still save their sponsors if she pretends she is amused by it. The sun is strong, and she tries out the sunglasses, but they make her vision odd, so she takes them off.

With her dehydration becoming serious, Katniss finds a berry bush, and only close examination and memory of her recent edible plants training convinces her to throw them away. By nightfall, she still hasn't found water, and is seriously fatigued. The report shows that only the tribute that Peeta killed has died during the second day. Katniss sleeps in a tree again, but by morning she has a headache and trouble thinking. She wonders why Haymitch hasn't sent her water and concludes that he is sending her a message by withholding a gift—a message that water is near. So she keeps looking, but with the hot afternoon, she feels she's near death. She finally falls, unable to rise, and decides that she is in a good place to die, when she realizes that her hands are in the mud and mud means water. It takes a lot of willpower for her to wait for the iodine to purify the water so it's safe to drink, but she manages, as best as she can tell, and rehydrates slowly to be safe. After drinking a gallon, she prepares another bottle, settles in a tree, eats rabbit and a cracker, and begins to feel better. She plans to camouflage her backpack and go fishing the following day. Several hours later, she is startled awake by a stampede, and looks around to see a wall of fire advancing toward her.

The Hunger Games: A Teaching Guide 51

Chapter 13   On Fire; Treed

Vocabulary

snarled 172 tangled
underbrush 172 plants under large trees
keep apace with 172 keep up with
suffocate 172 kill by stopping the breath
verging 173 bordering
flush out 173 force to come out of hiding
quell 173 overcome
outcropping 173 rock above the soil level
retch 174 throw up; vomit
indefinitely 174 forever
inferno 174 a place of fiery destructio
circuitous 174 roundabout; indirect
pillar 175 tall candle-shaped formation
launcher 175 device to launch a missile
overdrive 175 above the normal operating state
rigged 175 set w/ hidden traps
vipers 175 venomous snakes
abate 176 lessen; diminish
convulses 176 suffers muscle spasms
singed 176 burnt
fumbles 176 moves uncertainly

transformation 176 striking change
stifles 176 puts out; quenches; extinguishes
manipulate 177 force in an indirect way
crevice 178 narrow crack
blissfully 178 joyfully
gruesome 179 causing horror and distress
rebounds 180 comes back
rehydrate 180 recover from dehydration
unscathed 180 undamaged
intact 180 in one piece; whole
stupor 180 state of diminished senses
raspy 181 rough; grating
consolation 181 comfort
intentionally 182 purposely
scurry 182 hurry; race
flailing 182 swinging arms and legs wildly
conspiratorially 183 as if creating a sinister plan
potency 183 power
drizzle 183 trickle
bravado 183 show of courage
possum 183 short for opossum,

Journal and Discussion Questions

1. Draw parallels between Chapter 13 and Chapter 5.
2. There are three apparent allusions in this chapter on pp. 174–5: "inferno," "pillar of fir ," and "pit of vipers." Look them up and offer an explanation for them.
3. List examples of the narrative relying on Katniss being able to read the intentions of people outside the arena. Do you think this is realistic? Why or why not?
4. Summarize the chapter by making a flow hart that shows the interactions.

Summary

    Rushing to escape, Katniss unbuckles her sleeping bag and falls to the ground, following the fleeing animals until they outpace her. The heat is terrible, the smoke suffocating, and Katniss realizes that the fire is meant to force tributes together so the Games won't get boring. As she hurdles over a burning log, her jacket catches fir , and she stamps out the flame . The smoke is making her sick, and she shelters behind a rocky outcrop to vomit. As she considers looping back behind the fir , the first fireball hits a rock about two feet from her head, and she's fleeing again, dodging and ducking with each warning hiss. After some time, she begins retching again as the attack abates. She misses a warning hiss, and a fireball slides across her right calf. She puts out the fire by rolling her leg on the ground, but in tearing away the fabric, she burns her hands. In agony, she ponders the irony of Cinna's vision of her as the girl on fir . But the attack is over, though the wall of flames remains. Katniss moves on until she walks into a spring-fed pool. She soaks her hands and her leg, after almost fainting from seeing it. She considers whether she ought to move, but the pain is so intense when she takes her leg out of the water that she decides to stay, using the time to arrange her supplies, cut off the damaged part of her jacket, and eat some edible water plants, before falling asleep.

    When the Careers catch up, she has less than a minute's head start and is slowed by her injured leg. She chooses a high tree and climbs up 20 feet by the time the five Careers and Peeta arrive. She greets them cheerily and tauntingly invites them up. Cato starts climbing with his sword, as Katniss climbs higher, to about 50 feet. His weight breaks the branch he's on, and he falls, but isn't injured. Glimmer, who has the silver bow and arrows, climbs, while Katniss moves to 80 feet up. When Glimmer tries to shoot her and misses, Katniss grabs the arrow and waves it around tauntingly. The pack has a conference, and Peeta says they should deal with Katniss in the morning, because she's stuck and can't go anywhere. So Katniss moves to a steady fork and belts herself in, realizing how weak she is from pain and hunger. Suddenly, she thinks she sees an animal's eyes in a neighboring tree, but then realizes they are human eyes and belong to Rue, who points to something above Katniss's head.

Chapter 14

Tracker Jackers; the Silver Bow; Peeta Saves Katniss

Chapter 14 Page 185

Vocabulary

spawned 185 produced
strategically 185 for greatest effect
distinctive 185 recognizable
tolerate 185 handle; endure
hallucinations 185 sensory experiences of things that do not exist
venom 185 poison in their stings
formulated 186 came up with
vibration 186 shaking
precariously 187 dangerously
persevere 187 stick to it; persist
subdued 187 less lively/active than usual
sedated 187 made sleepy
groove 187 notch
sated 187 satisfie
treed 187 driven up a tree by pursuers
groggy 187 dazed
ointment 188 a soft, oily spread for healing
fend for 188 MM provide for
astronomical 188 enormously high
balm 188 a sweet-smelling ointment
reposition 188 adjust the placement of
inflamed 188 tender and painful

penetrate 189 see into
a cinch 189 easy
honing in 190 moving towards a goal
woozy 190 dizzy and dazed
mayhem 190 chaos
in pursuit 191 following
scamper 191 climb quickly and lightly
submerge 191 plunge; immerse
disfigured 191 made ugly; damaged
befuddled 191 confused
teetering 191 moving unsteadily
coma 192 lengthy state of unconsciousness
eradicated 192 wiped out
spewing 192 ejecting in a spray
putrid 192 in a state of foul decay
disintegrates 192 comes apart
lurch 192 move abruptly and awkwardly
hyperventilating 193 breathing abnormally fast, causing faintness
poised 193 in position; ready
uncomprehendingly 193 w/out being able to understand
disoriented 194 confused

Journal and Discussion Questions

1. What did you first think as Rue's reason for pointing out the nest to Katniss?
2. Explain the state of technological development in Panem.
3. What do you think was real in Katniss's report of getting the bow and the aftermath, and what do you think was the result of hallucination?
4. Summarize the chapter from Peeta's point of view.

Summary

Following Rue's gesture, Katniss makes out a wasp nest. She surmises that the wasps are one of the Capitol's muttations called tracker jackers, which hunt down anyone who disturbs their nest and whose poison can cause hallucinations and death, as well as huge swellings. Katniss formulates a plan to knock the nest on the tributes camped below her by sawing through the branch it's attached to. She'll have to hide the noise of sawing from the tributes as well as avoid alarming the wasps. She decides to saw during the anthem, and notes that the wasps are sedated by the smoke. She has not sawed through when the anthem ends, so she decides to finish the job at d wn.

Returning to her fork, she finds a silver parachute that signals a gift from a sponsor, with a little pot of powerful burn ointment attached; it eases the pain enough that she can sleep. Awakening at dawn, she treats her burns, packs her belongings, and notes that Glimmer, the apparent sentry for the pack, has fallen asleep. She signals to Rue so she can escape, and climbs up to finish sawing, but suffers three stings before she drops the nest. Quickly pulling out the stingers, she's still made woozy by the venom. Most of the tributes on the ground run for the lake; but two of the three girls, including Glimmer, are badly stung, and Katniss sees Glimmer fall to the ground, dying. With the coast clear, Katniss gets down the tree and back to her pool, where she submerges herself, but suddenly remembers the bow. She heads back, knowing that as soon as Glimmer is dead, the hovercraft will come and the bow will be removed from the arena with her body. She reaches Glimmer just as the cannon fire , and hallucination make Glimmer appear incredibly repulsive. Katniss has to lift her to pull the quiver from under her, and it appears that Glimmer's flesh disintegrates. Having secured both the bow and quiver, she hears the pack returning. She tries to aim an arrow, but seeing three strings, she can't.

She looks up to see a spear aimed at her and a shocked Peeta holding it. He shoves her away from him, screaming, "Run!" as Cato comes up behind him, and Katniss runs away, past her pool and further into the woods, until she trips and falls. Her last clear thought as the hallucinations render her unconscious is that Peeta just saved her life.

The Hunger Games: A Teaching Guide 53

Strategy 16

Plot—Distinguishing Types of Conflict

Directions: First, read the information. Then, answer the question or questions.

Conflict is at the core of a story's plot. Conflict is both what makes us wonder if the protagonist will attain his or her goal and what adds suspense and excitement to stories. Often there is one overarching conflict that takes up much of the book and stands in the way of the protagonist's progress. But each chapter or scene in a story usually also has conflict on a smaller scale.

The struggles that a protagonist undergoes in a story can be either **internal** or **external** (or both). In an **internal** conflict the protagonist undergoes an interior struggle. He or she might have:

- conflicting desire,
- values that are at odds with each other,
- clashing personality traits, and/or
- conflicting motive.

An internal conflict takes place in the character's mind and heart. People often have internal conflict as they grow and develop from one stage in their lives to the next, so you will often find internal conflict in novels in which the protagonist is a teenager (although there are often external conflicts as well), and sometimes (though not always) coming to grips with romantic feelings is at the root of it. The struggle within Katniss about her feelings for Gale, on the one hand, and her feelings for Peeta, on the other, is an ongoing topic in this novel. Internal conflict can also result from tyranny, oppression or terrorism, any of which can put a character's desires at odds with how he or she must behave, and this is another issue Katniss faces.

In an **external** conflict the protagonist struggles with something or someone outside of himself or herself. The conflict may be with:

- another individual,
- a challenging or complex task or problem,
- society,
- nature,
- an idea, or
- a force, such as good or evil.

The first external conflict that Katniss reports is with Buttercup, a cat she tried to drown, but that's only the first of many conflicts she reports, and it's a minor issue compared to the conflicts faced in the arena. It does, however, introduce life-and-death battles from the very first page, and the first conflic reported in a story can often provide insight about what is to come.

1. What appear to be the overarching goals in this story? Cite evidence to support your conclusion.
2. Skim Chapters 4–14 to find the conflicts that put the goals in jeo ardy and make a chart to show them. Then, as you continue reading, make entries for each new chapter. You may want to use the following format to show who Katniss is in conflict with (using *v.* for *versus*) and indicating what the conflict is about in parenthesis

Katniss/Peeta v. Haymitch (sober mentoring)

54   *The Hunger Games: A Teaching Guide*

Chapter 15

An Ally and a Plan

Chapter 15
Page 195

Vocabulary

manifest 195 appear (to me)
onslaught 195 attack
imagery 195 appearance of things that are not real; hallucinations
wracked 195 damaged
fetal position 195 curled posture resembling that of a baby in the womb
inventory 195 a complete, detailed listing
pervades 196 spreads throughout
stamen 196 part of a flower w/ the polle
nectar 196 secretion of a plant that attracts insects to pollinate the flowe
initiated 197 started
incident 197 happening
noxious 197 harmful to health
perspective 197 way of looking at the world
prominent 198 visible; sticking out
surreal 198 unreal; like a hallucination
abrupt 198 sudden
sufficient 198 enough
ally 200 teammate
tentatively 200 w/ hesitation
leaching 201 draining away
parsnip 201 a white, edible carrot-shaped root
ridiculed 203 mocked; made fun of
quotas 203 production requirements
haven 204 place of shelter
taking a cue 205 getting the idea
flare up 205 get worse

Journal and Discussion Questions

1. What is similar in Katniss's sighting of the dandelions when her family was starving and her acquiring the bow and arrows in the arena?
2. Explain why you do or don't think an alliance with Rue is good for Katniss.
3. What is the one difference of opinion that Rue and Katniss have?
4. How is Katniss's thinking different in this chapter compared to earlier?
5. Speculate about what you think Katniss's plan might be.
6. Summarize the chapter from Rue's point of view.

Summary

The tracker jacker venom gives Katniss hideous nightmares. When they have finally run their course, she does not know how long she's been where she is or what happened to the other members of the pack. She thinks of Gale, but her recollection is interrupted by the memory that Peeta saved her life, she thinks, acknowledging that by the time he arrived, she didn't know what was real. She wonders what Gale thought of it, and pushes the thought from her mind. The bow and arrows are real, and she feels they significantly raise her chances of winning the Games. She treats her burns, and tries some ointment on the stings, but it doesn't help. Dehydrated, she decides that she needs water first As she looks for water, she kills a rabbit, and then finds a stream, where she washes herself and her clothes, purifies more water, and eats a cracker and a beef strip. Following the stream, she shoots a bird that looks like a wild turkey, and is just starting to cook it, when she hears a twig snap.

It takes her a few moments to spot the tip of a child-sized boot behind a tree trunk, and—recognizing Rue—she calls out that the Careers aren't the only ones who can form alliances. Rue can't believe at first that Katniss wants her for an ally, but quickly comes forward and offers to fix her stings with leaves that she's gathered. After Rue's chewed them and applied them to the stings, Katniss feels much better. The girls come to an agreement, ignoring that it must be temporary. They share a meal including the bird—which Rue identifies as groosling—and then lay out all their food so they can plan, with Rue showing Katniss a new (to her) type of edible berry. Then they lay out their other gear, and Rue recognizes the "sunglasses" as night-vision glasses to see in the dark. When night comes, they head for a tree fork and share the sleeping bag. Rue tells Katniss that she was unconscious for two days and that only the two girls attacked by wasps died in that time. Katniss tells Rue that she thinks Peeta saved her life, and Rue confirms that he is not with the Careers now, and suggests that maybe he had to run after saving her. Katniss says it was probably part of his act to make people think he loves her, and Rue replies that she didn't think it was an act.

Rue mentions how strong the Careers are and Katniss tries to convince Rue that she and Rue are strong in a different way than the Careers. Rue points out that the Careers have all the supplies to aid them, and that gives Katniss the idea of considering how they would manage without the supplies, and she starts to formulate a plan to change the Careers' fortunes.

The Hunger Games: A Teaching Guide 55

Writer's Forum 4

Writing First-Person Narration

Directions: First, read the information. Then, answer the question or questions.

There's nothing like first-person present-tense narration for creating a sense of immediacy. It also ups the suspense and drama when the narrator is in danger. But besides its particular strengths, first-person narration has limitations that challenge even experienced authors like Collins.

Commentating One's Own Life

The blow-by-blow descriptions used by radio sports reporters, whose listeners have to rely on verbal description to know what's going on, is called *commentating*. Commentating gets awkward when used by a first-person narrator: "Somehow, through the smoke and vomit, I pick up the scent of singed hair." (p. 176). Even Twitter fanatics don't tell as many details about themselves as Katniss does. First-person point of view (POV) is less awkward when it focuses on other people or the narrator's past.

Intimacy and Choice of Assumed Audience

Who is Katniss talking to? It's not Collins's audience—you and me, reading the book: it's too intimate to be designed for strangers. It's not herself—one doesn't tell oneself things like "In a matter of minutes, my throat and nose are burning" (p. 173). It's not a record for those close to her—she'd use second person when speaking of them. In fact, the audience seems to be an unidentifiable construct The question is, do you think it works?

Limited by the Viewpoint, but Pretending Not to Be

In the arena, Katniss has no access to information from outside, and that's a problem for this plot. Collins has her speak with assurance about, for example, what the cameras are doing ("The minute I hit the ground, I'm guaranteed a close-up," p. 163) and what the audience, sponsors, Gamemakers, and Haymitch are thinking. Is Collins successful in convincing you?

I - I - I - I

With a first-person narrator talking about him- or herself, the first-peson singular pronoun (*I*) can get ridiculously overused. This can be softened by sometimes using constructions with *my* or *me* instead of *I* or balanced by reports of and reflections on others' actions and word .

The Unreliable Narrator

The trickiest type of narrator to convey is the one who's unreliable, whom the reader can't completely trust for information. Given that Katniss can come up with two opposing views of Peeta in a heartbeat, we know that her views aren't always accurate. She also fails to pick up on the meaning of some things that may seem obvious to us, and Collins has her omit things when it serves the narrative (like the contents of her plan with Rue). This builds suspense for the reader but changes the level of detail in the narration. This is another reason to keep assessing the narrative's believability.

There are several reasons to question the text inherent in the narration choice. It's good to start off trying to make sense of things as stated. Only if this doesn't work and there's sufficient evidence should you question the narrator's truth or the author's authority and choices.

1. Choose an appropriate real or imaginary incident to convey using a first-person present-tense narrator. When you're done, write a paragraph explaining the choices you made to make the most of the POV.

Chapter 16

Katnisses Loses Her Hearing; Rue in Trouble

Chapter 16
Page 208

Vocabulary

motivated 207 driven or urged on by
wholeheartedly 208 completely
misgivings 208 doubts
needling 208 bothering; annoying
distracted 208 unfocused
glint 210 spark
ordeal 210 trial; challenge
observant 210 watchful; noticing
stash 210 collection made for safekeeping
devise 211 plan
obliging 211 willing to work w/ others
rendezvous 213 meet at agreed time/place
replenish 214 fill up agai
reverting 214 returning to its former state
proximity 214 nearness
vicinity 214 area; region
copse 214 a thicket of bushes or small trees
domineering 215 bossy; controlling
ineffective 215 useless; not helpful
booby-trapped 216 rigged w/ hidden explosives
mulling over 216 thinking about
in the dark 217 lacking knowledge
accomplice 217 partner in wrongdoing
wily 218 crafty, cunning
dexterity 218 skill in movement; agility
reactivate 219 get something working again
demolishing 220 destroying completely
meticulous 220 very careful

Journal and Discussion Questions

1. How does Katniss's plan turn one of the Career's strengths into a weakness?
2. Explain why neither Katniss nor Rue could have destroyed the supplies alone?
3. How does Foxface inadvertently help Katniss?
4. Summarize the chapter by creating a timeline of Rue's, Katniss's, Foxface's, and the Career Packs' actions.

Summary

Setting aside the fact that she and Rue can't both win the Games, and with Rue snuggled against her, Katniss falls asleep considering how difficult it would likely be for the Careers to feed themselves without the supplies. She is awakened by the cannon and wonders who died. Rue is already up and has eggs for their breakfast. They go hunting, and Katniss collects information from Rue, who has been spying on the Careers. The most puzzling thing she's seen is that the boy from District 3, who is not a Career tribute, is working with them, staying at the camp full time, guarding the supplies, but without any weapons that Rue could see. As they gather food, a plan emerges.

They collect wood and build two diversionary campfires—Rue will do a third on her own. They divide the food and plan a rendezvous, and Katniss leaves Rue with the sleeping bag. Rue teaches Katniss her mockingjay song, so she can let Katniss know she's okay if she can't get to the rendezvous. They hug and wish each other luck. As she starts off, Katniss connects Rue and Prim in her thoughts, but then realizes that while Prim has their mother, Gale, and the baker to look after her, Rue only has Katniss.

Katniss follows Rue's directions to the best place from which to spy on the Career's camp—a copse with thick, concealing foliage at the edge of the woods. She spots four tributes: three Careers and the boy from District 3. The Cornucopia has been emptied, and the supplies piled in a pyramid, except for some that are sitting around the edges. The pyramid is covered with netting, and Katniss concludes that it's booby-trapped, but she's not sure how. Just then, she sees Cato pointing to the woods behind her, and knows that Rue has lit the first fir . Katniss can hear the Careers argue about whether the District 3 boy should come with them. Cato says the boy's job at the camp is done and they need him in the woods. The boy from District 1 asks about "Lover Boy," and Cato says he told them to forget Peeta, who he expects to bleed to death. Cato's last audible words as the group heads into the woods are a threat to kill Katniss in his "own way."

Katniss has just decided to move in closer, when Foxface appears and delicately picks a path to the pyramid, revealing to Katniss that the ground is mined. Foxface steals small amounts from several places, but not enough to be noticeable, and then escapes into the woods. Katniss reasons that the District 3 boy reactivated the mines that stood around the launch plates when the tributes first came into the arena. She tries to imagine how he would have arranged them and how she can set off enough to do serious damage and leave no trace of her arrow. After Rue's second fire has been lit, Katniss realizes freeing apples in a burlap sack can trigger the mines. It takes three arrows to tear open the bag, spilling the apples to the ground and setting off an explosion that blows her backward.

The Hunger Games: A Teaching Guide

Chapter 17

Chapter 17 Page 222

Katnisses Loses Her Hearing; Rue in Trouble

Vocabulary

debris 222 rubble from something ruined
activate 222 set off
acrid 222 irritating, burning, or stinging
salvage 222 save; rescue
insufficient 222 not enough
doggedly 223 w/ stubborn dedication
nick of time 223 the last possible moment
fractured 223 split; broken into fragments
distorted 227 not natural; strange; odd
enlist 227 gain

famished 228 extremely hungry
invigorating 228 filling w/ energ
diminishes 228 lessens
undetectable 228 not able to be noticed
tromping 229 walking w/ heaving steps
lopsided 229 one-sided; unbalanced
deflated 229 reduced in size
prospects 230 likelihood of success
decadent 230 excessively expensive
interspersed 231 placed at intervals

Journal and Discussion Questions

1. Explain why the loss of her hearing is such a blow to Katniss.
2. How would you judge the success of the plan, given Cato's response?
3. What incorrect conclusion do the Careers draw?
4. What does Foxface's success in salvaging things suggest about her? About the Careers?
5. Look up *interspersed* in the dictionary. How is Collins's use different?
6. Why do you think, with Katniss bearing down, the attacker speared Rue?
7. Graph this chapter where y-axis = Katniss's hope/fear and x-axis = time.

Summary

Hitting the ground hard, Katniss has the wind knocked out of her. Deafened, she feels the ground shaking with repeated explosions, as she uses her arms to shield her face from flying debris. After about a minute, the ground stops shaking, though smoke fills the air. A glance at the destruction assures Katniss that there isn't anything to salvage. Realizing that she'd better escape, Katniss finds she's incredibly dizzy, and when she doesn't regain her stability in a few minutes, she starts to panic. She finds that her left ear is bloody, and though she is terrified of being deaf, she is sure that she is on-screen and so, mustn't let her fear show. She pulls up her jacket hood and ties it to prevent a blood trail, and finds that—though she cannot walk—she can crawl. Although she is knocked down by a couple of stray mine blasts, she gets back to the copse just as Cato comes running onto the scene and throws a tantrum. The boy from District 3 throws stones into the wreckage to make sure all the mines have been activated, and then the pack examines the damage, finding nothing of value. Cato kills the District 3 boy, but the other two Careers convince Cato that the person who destroyed the supplies is dead and that they missed the cannon shot in the explosions. When the nightly report shows that only the two boys from Districts 3 and 10—whom Katniss assumes died in the morning—have died, the Careers know that the bomber survived. They put on their night-vision glasses, make a torch from a tree branch, and head into the woods.

By this time, Katniss is able to hear a ringing in her right ear, giving her hope that her hearing is returning. She stays still for a few hours, figuring her current spot is safe, with the Careers heading into the woods. She puts on her night-vision glasses and determines that there are just eight tributes left. The night gets cold, and Katniss is freezing without the sleeping bag. She covers herself with leaves, pine needles, and her plastic sheeting, and manages to sleep. When she wakes, it's already light, and she hears a laugh, signaling regained hearing in her right ear, though it is still ringing. She sees Foxface, who—more careful than the Careers—manages to salvage some useful items in the ruins. Katniss acknowledges Foxface's intelligence and considers enlisting her as another ally, but decides against it since she doesn't trust her.

Although the Careers have not returned, Katniss sets off to meet Rue, walking barefoot in the streambed to hide her tracks and shooting two fish Rue is not yet at the rendezvous point, and Katniss concludes that she's being cautious and settles in to wait, attending to her various wounds and then climbing a tree. When late afternoon arrives without Rue's return, Katniss decides to go looking for her, but leaves a few mint leaves as a sign that she's been there. As she stealthily slips through the trees, she hears a mockingjay sing Rue's four-note tun. Happily, she follows the sound. Suddenly, she hears Rue scream and call her name. Katniss runs, even though she realizes it may be a trap, calling to Rue that she's coming. Breaking into a clearing, Katniss finds Rue caught in a net, and just as she reaches out to Katniss, a spear goes through her.

58 *The Hunger Games: A Teaching Guide*

Strategy 17

Engaging with a Text Through Imaging

Directions: First, read the information. Then, answer the question or questions.

The meaning of a work of literature is felt by readers as they enter into the story in their imaginations. In the act of reading, the words of a book are translated into experience by the reader, experience that for many readers can include **imaging** (sight, sound, touch, etc.) and feelings.

Writing instructor Janet Burroway explains that "Fiction tries to reproduce the emotional impact of experience. And this is a more difficult task, because written words are symbols representing sounds, and the sounds themselves are symbols representing things, actions, qualities, spatial relationships, and so on. Written words are thus at two removes from experience. Unlike the images of film and drama, which directly strike the eye and ear, they are transmitted first to the mind, where they must be translated into images [by the reader]" (*Writing Fiction: A Guide to Narrative Craft*, sixth edition, New York: Longman, 2002, p. 54).

Different texts foster different amounts and different kinds of imagery and feeling (also called "affect"). In part, these differences can result from the author's use of more or less description and more or less sensory language, the author's focus on abstractions or concrete topics, a very complex or a simpler writing style, academic or ordinary diction, and so on. As a result, your imaging won't always be exactly the same, and different senses may be emphasized at different times. Even when your imaging is at its most vivid, it is likely that it will not be as specific as a photograph or movie is. The visual images we create in our minds are characteristically not sharp and finely focused, a quality that literary critic Wolfgang Iser calls "optical poverty." This is an important point because you shouldn't expect these images to be something they're not or force them into a mold. Just let them come into your head, experience them, and take note.

Sensory language engages the senses of sight, hearing, smell, taste, and touch, by fostering images that appeal to the senses. Sight is the sense most often invoked, and taste, usually the least. Sensory language helps readers imagine the scene in the "movie" in their minds. It helps bring the black and white of the printed or digital book to life.

Sometimes a writer will emphasize one or two particular senses. As Katniss approaches the Careers' camp in Chapter 16, she says her senses are sharpened, and her following observations emphasize the senses of both sight and hearing. This forms a contrast with Katniss's inability to hear in the beginning of Chapter 17 and her "fractured" vision when she awakens still wearing the night-vision glasses. These are two cases in which the plot is calling attention to the sensory world.

1. Make a list of incidents in the arena so far in which hearing has been critical to Katniss.

2. Identify at least two incident descriptions prior to the arena and two in the arena that appeal to the senses of touch. Then do the same for taste.

3. To keep track of your imaging, it is useful to write about or draw what you've seen. Don't worry about your drawing ability; just do the best you can in whatever medium is most comfortable for you or best conveys what you want to communicate or recollect about your experience. Create a record for Chapters 1 through 17 now, and add to it each time you complete another chapter.

The Hunger Games: A Teaching Guide 59

Strategy 18

Understanding Cliffhangers

Directions: First, read the information. Then, answer the question or questions.

The term *cliffhanger* may have arisen from an actual incident in a serial novel by Thomas Hardy, *A Pair of Blue Eyes*, in which a character was left hanging by his fingertips from the edge of a cliff at the end of an episode.

A cliffhanger is a way of handling the temporary ending in a narrative that is going to be continued. The break in the narrative can be a television show pausing for commercial break; the last episode in a television series's season; the gap between sections of a serial novel, the delay between publication dates of novels in a series, or the page turn between chapters in a print or digital edition of a novel. The cliffhanger generally leaves the protagonist or another major character in peril or provides (or hints at) a major revelation. All will be revealed . . . but not until after the break.

Creating a cliffhanger is a narrative strategy. It helps build suspense. It makes the audience long for the next portion. It encourages the audience to think about the story even when they're not actively engaged with it. During the break—even if it's just turning the page to the next chapter—there is time to wonder, to predict, to express one's opinion on social media, etc. If the writer did a good job, when the narrative returns, the audience is dying to jump back in.

Cliffhangers are more common in genres that rely heavily on suspense and danger: action, adventure, horror, science fiction crime, mysteries, and thrillers. It is used in other genres as well. But not every temporary ending is a cliffhanger, even in the genres in which it is most often used. For one thing, even the longest series may get to a point at which the end is the real, final ultimate end, and—except in very special cases—this ending is not a cliffhanger.

In *The Hunger Games*, the first chapter ends with a major revelation: the name of the girl tribute for District 12 for the 74th Hunger Games. The reader is almost forced to wonder what Katniss will do. Even if we know already that Katniss, rather than her sister, is going to be in the Games, we are likely to wonder how she will be able to manage this. This is definitely a cliffhanger.

At the end of chapter two, in contrast, Katniss refers to Effie Trinket's statement about the odds being in one's favor in a way that sums up the occurrences of the first two chapters. This is a different kind of chapter ending. We don't know what will come next, and the reiteration of a thought from earlier is a hint to the reader to look back and reassess, not chomp at the bit to keep moving ahead.

As you read, your own reactions can inform you about what types of chapter endings the writer is using: if what you just read leaves you dying to see what comes next, you may simply be highly engaged in the story, or you be dealing with cliffhangers. When you feel this, you can be alerted to keep an eye on how the author is shaping your reading experience.

1. For Chapters 3–17, identify and describe the cliffhangers you find Then describe the endings that function differently, by rounding out an incident or inviting a review of went before, for example.

The Hunger Games: A Teaching Guide

Chapter 18   Rue's Death; Rule Change

Vocabulary

embedded 233 firmly set in plac
fretful 234 irritable; quick to whimper
soothing 234 relieving pain; sweet
eerily 235 mysteriously; strangely
ravings 236 wild, irrational talk or yelling
inflict 236 impose; force
impotence 236 inability to act successfully
tremor 238 shaking
despondency 238 deep sadness
authorized 239 gave permission to
decked 239 decorated; adorned
melodic 240 musical; sweet-sounding
infuses 240 fills penetrates
unblinkingly 240 w/out blinking
lethargy 240 lack of energy and motivation
robotic 240 automatic; mechanical
consolidate 241 organize wanted items, while discarding unwanted items
bearings 241 sense of one's location
avenge 242 cause harm in return for harm caused to oneself or another
banish 243 drive away; expel
scarce 244 hard to get; limited
inducement 244 motivation

Journal and Discussion Questions

1. Compare and contrast Katniss's relationships with Prim and Rue.
2. Do you buy Katniss saying "Prim" when she means "Rue"? Explain.
3. What do you think is the wider significance of District 11's gift?
4. Katniss suddenly wants to talk to Peeta. Why?
5. Summarize the context of Katniss's first kill in the arena including the circumstances, her motivation, and her reaction. Use the Choice Analysis Tool.

Summary

Katniss immediately shoots dead the boy from District 1, who speared Rue. Rue indicates that there are no more attackers, and Katniss cuts her out of the net. Realizing that Rue's wound is fatal, Katniss takes her hand and tells Rue that she blew up the food. She promises that she will win for both of them. A cannon fires for the boy, and Rue asks her not to leave and to sing to her. Katniss takes Rue's head in her lap and sings a song she used to sing to Prim, and the mockingjays pick it up. The cannon fires for Rue, but Katniss does not leave. She kisses Rue on the forehead and lays her head back on the ground. Then she collects the District 1 boy's pack, the arrow that killed him, and Rue's pack. She realizes that she doesn't hate the boy, but the Capitol. Thinking of Gale's railings against the Capitol, she feels impotent. But then, recalling Peeta's words on the roof, she wants to show that both she and Rue are more than just pawns in the Capitol's Games. She plucks an armful of wildflowers and arranges them over Rue's body. Then she gives Rue the District 12 salute and walks away, not looking back as the hovercraft takes Rue's body. A mockingjay begins to sing Rue's melody that means she's safe, and Katniss reflects that she is good and safe no .

Without Rue, Katniss loses her sense of purpose and wanders aimlessly until sunset, ready to kill any Career she sees. As she prepares to bed down, she spots a silver parachute and discovers that it's a loaf of bread from Rue's district. Realizing that the gift must have been intended for Rue and authorized for her as a thank you from District 11 after Rue died, Katniss is deeply moved and thanks District 11 aloud. She knows that it is the first time a district's people have ever given a gift to a tribute that was not theirs. The nightly recap shows only the known two dead, leaving six tributes. Belted to a branch high up in a tree, Katniss has happy dreams of Rue, but in the morning, she's lost the will to act. Only the thought of Prim watching her gives her the strength to force herself into action. She reviews her supplies, which now include a first-aid kit, and decides she must hunt. Having lost her bearings, she tries to head towards the stream.

She shoots three grooslings and uses the unlit signal fire to cook them. As they roast, she wonders whether the Careers have figured out that she was the one who both destroyed the supplies and killed the boy from District 1. She wishes she could tell Peeta about Rue's flowers and that she now understands what he meant on the roof. She renews her commitment to avenge Rue and believes she can do it. She wraps up her food, heads for the stream, and gets set for the night early, only then realizing that the boy from District 1 was her first kill. She remembers Gale's remark about the similarity with hunting, but concludes that only the execution is similar. The recap shows that no one has died, and she has covered her good ear to shut out the anthem and sleep, when trumpets blare. The announcer congratulates the six remaining tributes and announces a rule change: if both tributes from one district are the last two alive, they will both be declared winners. Unable to stop herself, Katniss blurts out Peeta's name.

The Hunger Games: A Teaching Guide   61

Strategy 19 — Analyzing Lyrics

Directions: First, read the information. Then, answer the question or questions.

Poetry and song lyrics make meaning through the order and patterning of sound. They appeal to the senses and make the most of every sound, syllable, and word. Even though poetry and song lyrics are not exactly the same thing, because the song lyrics in *The Hunger Games* are presented without music, analyzing them as a poem is the best we can do. Knowing a little about poetic structures, rhythm and meter, and sound devices, including rhyme, will help you understand them.

Verses of a traditional song, such as a lullaby, are typically each sung once, while the **chorus** is a section that is repeated, often between each verse. Katniss's song has two verses and a chorus that she sings twice.

Stanza is the name for a stand-alone division of a poem or song. A stanza with two lines is called a *couplet*, while one with four lines is called a *quatrain*. In the lullaby Katniss sings to Rue, each of the stanzas is a quatrain made up of two rhyming couplets.

Rhyme, the use of repeated sounds, is the sound device that is most closely associated with poetry. Rhyme can be categorized by the type of sounds that are repeated and the placement of the words that rhyme. In the two verses, each of which begins with the words "Deep in the meadow," the two rhyming couplets end with different rhymes. In the chorus, all four of the lines rhyme with each other

There are three main **categories of rhyme**, which are partly differentiated by whether they fall on a stressed (strong) or unstressed (weak) syllable.

- **Identical rhyme** is rhyme in which the exact same word is repeated *Here/Here*
- **Perfect rhyme** is rhyme in which one or more syllables are repeated except for the initial sound. Perfect rhyme includes strong syllable rhyme: *ray/lay, when/again*; multiple syllable rhyme: *willow/pillow*; and rhyme of only the weak syllable: *meadow/willow*.
- **Near rhyme** is rhyme that doesn't meet the criteria for perfect rhyme, but has similar sounds nevertheless. The use of near rhyme can be intentional, chosen because the poet wanted that effect: it doesn't necessarily indicate a failure to find a perfect rhyme. Three widely used types of near rhyme are:

    1. **Assonance**, in which only the vowel sound in the stressed syllable of a word is repeated *safe/place*
    2. **Consonance**, in which only the final consonant sound is repeated *warm/harm*
    3. **Alliteration**, in which only the initial consonant sound is repeated *grass/green*

There are three main categories of **rhyme placement:**
- **End rhyme** is rhyme at the end of lines. It is the most often used.
- **Initial rhyme** is rhyme at the beginning of lines.
- **Medial rhyme** is rhyme between a word somewhere in the middle of the line with another word, which may be in three different places:

    1. at the end of the same line (called **internal rhyme**)
    2. somewhere in the middle of the same line (called **close rhyme**)

3. in the middle of a line before or after the first rhyme word (**interlaced rhyme**)

Here is a chart that shows the placement and category of each type of rhyme that appears in the lullaby. The words that rhyme are bold-faced:

RHYME TYPES	
Placement/Rhyme Type	Example
End rhyme/ Consonance	Here it's safe, here it's **warm** Here the daisies guard you from every **harm**
Initial rhyme/ Identical rhyme	**Here** it's safe, here it's warm **Here** the daisies guard you from every harm
Internal rhyme/ Alliteration	A bed of **grass**, a soft **green** pillow
Close rhyme/ Perfect rhyme	And **when again** they open, the sun will rise
Interlaced rhyme/ Assonance	Here it's **safe**, here it's warm ... Here is the **place** where I love you

A song's content is a useful starting point for analysis. What is the song about? After determining the subject, note the structure, including the use of stanzas (if any) and lines. Try reading the song aloud several times. It's a good idea to note the use of the various types of rhyme and other sound devices. You should also consider the grammar, syntax, and mechanics used in the lyrics. How do all these devices contribute to the meaning?

Since poetry and songs have ways of presenting sensitive and delicate emotions and experiences, they can be used to express things that are not as easily rendered in prose. In stories that are harsh and/or brutal, a song or poem can provide a contrast to the savage events and give the reader an emotional break from the fear, disgust, and other negative emotions that the main part of the text evokes.

1. Using the information in this lesson as a jumping off point, write an analysis of the song Katniss sings to Rue.
2. How does the song temporarily alter the mood?
3. Find the lyrics for another lullaby. Use the information presented here to analyze the use of rhyme.

Strategy 19, cont.

The Hunger Games: A Teaching Guide

Writer's Forum 5 — Writing Lyrics

Directions: First, read the information. Then, answer the question or questions.

Poet W. H. Auden spoke of poetry as a "game of knowledge, a bringing to consciousness, by naming them, of emotions and their hidden relationships."* And thinking of poetry or lyrics as a game we, as readers, play with the poet or we, as poets, play with our readers can help us understand a genre that no one can clearly defin , though many have tried.

The poet or lyricist gives readers and listeners sounds and sense set in a shape on a sheet of paper or in digital form. The sounds include rhythms and repetitions. Saying the poem aloud several times will help you discover its sounds, whether you are the reader or the poet. The sense includes literal and figurative language, sensory language, made-up words, onomatopoeia, double meanings and constructions that break the rules we usually follow for using language when we are writing prose. The shape on the page helps us know how to read the poem. We enter the game and see what happens; we play with the sense and sound to not only find but also to FEEL meaning. And when we write poetry, we turn this all around, becoming the maker of these experiences.

The relationship between sound and sense in each poem is unique, depending on the subject of the poem and the speaker. The poet may be, but often is not, the speaker in the poem. Lullabies, for example, are addressed to babies, and made so that the singer—whoever he or she is—can identify with the speaker, become the speaker, as the song quiets the child in his or her arms.

1. The anthem of Panem is mentioned several times, but the lyrics are not provided in this novel. An anthem is a patriotic song that praises one's country and usually includes pledges of devotion, as you can see in the national anthem of the United States, "The Star-Spangled Banner." You can find all four verses here

   http://www.thenationalanthemproject.org/lyrics.html

   Anthems are less likely than lullabies to have a full chorus, but in the "Star-Spangled Banner," you'll notice that every verse ends with repeated words that function like a chorus:

   > "……………………………………………………………………wave
   > O'er the land of the free and the home of the brave"

   Write at least three verses of lyrics for the Panem anthem. Make sure that it reflects views that are in keeping with what the Capitol would want citizens of Panem to sing. Choose either a full chorus or repeated words at the end of each verse, as in "The Star-Spangled Banner."

---

* "Poetry as a Game of Knowledge," from *Poets at Work*, ed. Charles D. Abbott, New York, 1948, pp. 171–81. Copyright 1948 by Harcourt, Brace & World, Inc.

Test: Chapters 10–18

Vocabulary

Look at each group of words. Tell why it is important in the story.

1. catacombs, syringe
2. bounty, serrated, iodine, radiating
3. retch, inferno, rehydrate
4. possum, vibration, groove
5. coma, spewing, putrid, disintegrates
6. copse, booby-trapped, rendezvous

Essay Topics

1. On p. 58, Haymitch offers Peeta and Katniss a very explicit deal in order for him to stay engaged in mentoring them. Does he stick to that deal once they're in the arena? Why do you think Haymitch makes that choice?

2. List situations in the novel in which the exercise of self-control has paid off.

3. Compare and contrast the arena experience with any a reality television show in which contestants face challenges by either watching at least one episode or researching the presentation of the show.

4. Identify the industries in Districts 1, 3, 4, 11, 12, and 13. Using an outline map of North America and the history of Panem in Chapter 1, draw your best estimation of the location of these districts and explain why you placed them as you did. Sample map: http://commons.wikimedia.org/wiki/File:North_america_blank_range_map.png

5. Review the contents of all the backpacks Katniss has collected and the use she has made of them so far. What predictions can you make for the plot based on the contents of the materials she has just acquired?

6. Is the reason Rue decides to trust Katniss significant? Explain your thinkin .

7. Why does Haymitch call Katniss *sweetheart*? Why does Peeta?

8. In Chapter 11, p. 150, Katniss says of the girl from District 2, "All the general fear I've been feeling condenses into an immediate fear of this girl, this predator who might kill me in seconds. How does this capture the experience of the Games for the tributes?

9. Create a 2-D map or 3-D model of the arena, based on what you have read so far. Add to it as you continue to read.

10. How has shooting fruit been important in the novel so far?

Chapter 19

PART III "THE VICTOR"
Finding Wounded Peeta; the Cave

Vocabulary

assailants 247 attackers
dissipate 247 disappear; evaporate
pariahs 247 outcasts
unprecedented 247 never done before
condemning 247 treating unfavorably
jeopardize 247 put at risk
ambush 249 attack from a hidden location
scrupulously 249 extremely
incapacitated 249 unable to act
ruse 250 trick
navigate 251 find one's way
hugging 251 keeping close to

faculties 251 powers; abilities
whip around 252 turn around quickly
peruse 252 examine carefully
levity 253 joking; treating things lightly
alleviate 254 lessen
festering 256 filled w/ pus rotting
fared 257 lasted; survived; managed
caliber 257 quality
revolting 257 disgusting
squeamish 258 easily disgusted
lethal 258 deadly

Journal and Discussion Questions

1. What is Katniss's motivation to seek out Peeta?
2. What do you think Peeta has done to keep the "star-crossed lovers" angle alive?
3. What clues lead Katniss to Peeta?
4. Where do Katniss and Peeta go for the night and why?
5. When Katniss says Peeta is "great at this stuff" (p. 261) what is she assuming?
6. Summarize how Katniss applies prior knowledge in this chapter.

Summary

Katniss covers her mouth too late: nearby frogs start croaking, and she expects to be attacked any moment before remembering that there's hardly anyone left Peeta has become her ally. Her doubts about him flee—not because she now trusts him, but because if they harmed each other now, they'd be outcasts when they got home, and she'd lose her sponsors. Reconsidering, she concludes that Peeta has been playing the love angle all along and the audience are so into it that the success of the Games would be jeopardized if the Gamemakers didn't acknowledge it. So, she reasons, whatever Peeta's done in the Games, the audience must be convinced that it was to keep Katniss alive, and therefore even joining forces with the Careers must have been to protect her. Katniss considers the remaining competition: Foxface, the boy from District 11, Thresh, and the two Careers from District 2, the only other tributes who benefit from the new rule. In the morning, Katniss tackles the problem of finding Peeta with the Careers knowing that she's seeking him. She wonders how he's stayed alive if he's as hurt as Cato thinks and figures he must be near water. Choosing the stream as the most likely site, she starts a fire as a ruse and begins searching, walking in the streambed. She spots some bloodstains, and risks saying his name, but a mockingjay picks up her tones, so she doesn't call again. Suddenly, she hears him ask if she's come to finish him off. But she can't see him until he opens his eyes and reveals how perfectly he's camouflaged himself in the riverbank.

Peeta tells Katniss that Cato's cut is high up his left leg, and she suggests getting him into the stream so she can wash him off and treat his wounds. This is harder than she expected because Peeta is too weak to move and her efforts hurt him, so he stays on the bank. She starts washing him off and treats his tracker jacker stings and a burn on his upper body, but realizes that he's burning with fever, so she gives him pills from the first-aid kit. When she gets his pants off, she can see that the wound is festering, and she's not really equipped to treat it. But she starts with the tracker jacker leaves, and this helps drain the pus, but also enables her to see that the cut goes to the bone. She then applies the burn ointment and puts a sterile bandage on it. When his clothes are clean and dry, they try to move to safety, but Peeta is too weak. They stop about 50 yards downstream, where Katniss has spotted a cavelike structure in the rocks about 20 yards away from the water. She layers the cave floor with pine needles and tucks Peeta into the sleeping bag, then builds a blind out of vines to hide the cave mouth.

Peeta thanks Katniss for finding him and starts to tell her something about if he doesn't make it back, but after trying twice to cut him off, she kisses him and forbids him to die. Stepping out of the cave, she finds a parachute with a pot of hot broth, and interprets this to mean that Haymitch will reward romance and if she wants more gifts, such as medicine for Peeta, she'd better appear more loving and give the audience what they want. So she kisses Peeta awake and shows him the broth that Haymitch has sent him.

66 *The Hunger Games: A Teaching Guide*

Writer's Forum 6 — Writing Description

Directions: First, read the information. Then, answer the question or questions.

In descriptive writing, writers share the attributes of something so readers can picture it in their mind's eye. As a writer, you choose the features to mention based on what stands out among the physical properties and internal attributes of whatever you are describing, and these features will be different depending on your subject. If you were describing a person, the features you would focus on would likely be among those discussed in Strategy 6 Interpreting Characterization, p. 22, but in describing objects, places, or ideas, you would choose different features, as appropriate.

There are some general questions you can use to help you formulate your description of an object, place, or idea, as applicable:

- What is its name, species, or type? What is it not?
- What are its attributes and/or parts?
- What is the experience of it like?—how does it look, smell, taste, feel, sound?
- How does it relate to other things in its environment or context?
- What are its possibilities and limitations?
- What is its current state? What is its history?
- How did it come to be?
- What is its value?

The way you organize the information in a description may vary depending on what you are describing. Organization can help convey meaning. You can organize your description in these ways, as appropriate:

- top to bottom
- front to back
- side to side
- around the perimeter
- inside, then outside, or vice versa
- from the beginning to the end of its cycle
- most important trait to least important
- least important trait to most important

Source words that can help you express concepts of similarity and diversity in your description include:

Similarity

- also
- and
- as well as
- similarly
- besides
- furthermore
- likewise
- alike
- in addition
- too
- at the same time
- resemble

Diversity/Dissimilarity

- differ
- whereas
- however
- while
- but
- on the contrary
- conversely
- though
- on the other hand

1. Which two senses does Katniss appeal to in the descriptions of herself, having blurted Peeta's name and the moment of spotting Peeta?
2. Reread the description of the fir , starting with "The world has transformed . . ." and ending with ". . . at any moment" (p. 172). Then describe some intense natural phenomenon you have experienced—a storm, getting caught in a wave, a blizzard—using some of the same techniques, as well as those described above.

The Hunger Games: A Teaching Guide   67

Chapter 20

Prim's Goat; Invitation to a Feast

Vocabulary

scant 262 bare
sheen 262 shine
tethered 263 tied or confined (figurativ
caresses 265 loving touches
potent 266 powerful
ratcheting 266 raising, degree by degree
mince 267 cut up in very small pieces
wheedles 268 persuade w/ flatter
huff 268 exhale a puff of air
exasperation 268 irritation
buck 269 male deer, sheep, goat, or rabbit
yearling 269 a deer in its second year
bidding 269 pledging money at an auction

intervened 269 interrupted
venison 270 flesh of deer used as foo
hacking MM 270 coughing harshly in spasms
mauled 270 injured
nanny 271 female goat
drily 273 w/ irony for humorous effect
stalemate 275 deadlock; standoff
reluctantly 275 w/out enthusiasm
rambles 275 talk w/out meaning or point
gaggle 276 group of silly people
addictive 276 habit-forming
consciousness 277 awareness of and responsiveness to surroundings

Journal and Discussion Questions

1. What evidence in Chapters 19 and 20 point to a camera and mic in the cave?
2. Peeta says Katniss is a terrible liar. Weigh the evidence and give an opinion.
3. Why does Peeta say he will follow Katniss if she goes to the feast?
4. What are Katniss's various motivations for trying to get to the feast?
5. Summarize the story of Lady, including the alternative beginning.

Summary

When the broth is gone, Katniss eats and watches the recap, while Peeta sleeps. Concerned about their proximity to his camouflage locale, she puts on her night-vision glasses and keeps guard. When it grows colder, she joins Peeta in the sleeping bag and realizes he's burning with fever. As she puts cool, wet compresses on his forehead, she becomes aware of what she's sacrificed in order to find and care for him, and hopes she made the right decision. Peeta's fever breaks, and Katniss goes to gather the safe berries to make a mash for him. He's worried when he awakes to find her absent. She catches him up on who's still alive and feeds him, and he keeps watch while she naps. But when she awakens, his fever is back, and they both realize that it's blood poisoning, which will kill him without proper care. They agree that he will simply have to outlive the others and be cured after they've won, and Katniss goes to the stream to make him some soup.

Peeta asks for a story of her happiest day. Katniss tells him of getting a birthday present for Prim, altering the facts to avoid getting people in District 12 in trouble. She tells how she and Gale went to the market on the square. She was planning to buy fabric for a dress until she saw that the Goat Man had an injured goat and decided she wanted it for Prim. Although the Goat Man said the goat was promised to the butcher, Rooba, when Rooba came, she realized Katniss wanted it and said the goat was too damaged to be any good to her. After Katniss and the Goat Man haggled to set a price, Katniss and Gale brought the goat home, and her mother and Prim healed it. Peeta says he can see why that made her happy, and Katniss refers to the money the goat earned. Peeta mocks her, since it's clear to him it was the joy she gave Prim that made her happy.

Katniss feels Peeta's hot forehead and lies, telling him he's a bit cooler. Just then the trumpets signal another special announcement. Katniss is prepared to ignore it, but the announcer says that tributes from each district will find what they need desperately in a marked backpack at the Cornucopia at dawn. Peeta insists she not risk her life for him. Katniss lies, saying she has no intention of going, but Peeta knows she is lying. Katniss retorts that he can't stop her, and he says he can follow her and call her name. Katniss asks if he expects her to let him die. He promises not to die if she promises not to go, and Katniss pretends to agree, making him promise to do everything she says. She brings in the soup, and Peeta eats it all but starts losing his grip on reality, and as Katniss washes the bowl in the stream, she thinks that if she doesn't get to the feast, Peeta will die. She almost misses the parachute, which she soon realizes is the sleep syrup that is common in District 12, and with which she can knock Peeta out long enough to attend the feast. She mashes berries and mint leaves with the syrup to disguise it, claiming it's "sugar berries," but on the last bite, Peeta recognizes it, and she has to force him to swallow. He loses consciousness, and she asks him, rhetorically, "Who can't lie?"

68 *The Hunger Games: A Teaching Guide*

Writer's Forum 7

Composing an Anecdote

Directions: First, read the information. Then, answer the question or questions.

An anecdote is a short, self-contained story that is usually interesting, humorous, or insightful. It can recount a true, real-life event, or its content may be fictional It would not be unusual to find anecdotes in biographies, autobiographies, and memoirs, but they also occur in fictional histories of any genre. Katniss's story of Peeta giving her the bread and her tale of acquiring Lady are both anecdotes.

Like any other narrative, an anecdote has a plot with a beginning, middle, and end. It also has characters, sometimes even a main character. Some anecdotes are almost entirely composed of dialogue between characters, but many are narratives—though unlike most narratives, they often do not have a well-developed setting and have very little, if any, character development.

Anecdotes are often centered on a single event or a sequence of events occurring over a relatively short period of time. In keeping with this, anecdotes—whether primarily dialogue or primarily narrative—are likely to have little description beyond whatever is necessary for setting up the story at the beginning. Also, unlike other types of narrative and dialogue, anecdotes are likely to have a lesson or a punchline, or some other fairly explicit way of stating what the point is. And there usually isn't much room for varied interpretation of that point, although Katniss and Peeta disagree about the point of the anecdote about Lady.

1. Rewrite material from *The Hunger Games* to create an anecdote about Peeta's artistic abilities in frosting and camouflag , beginning with the material in the Training Center (Chapter 7) and ending with Peeta revealing himself to Katniss as he lies camouflaged in the riverbank (Chapter 19). Write it from Katniss's perspective, as an anecdote she makes up for herself as she's keeping watch while awaiting the feast at the Cornucopia. To review the rules for punctuating dialogue, see Writer's Forum 3: Writing Dialogue, p. 50.

The Hunger Games: A Teaching Guide 69

Chapter 21

The Gamemaker's Feast; Death and Medicine

Vocabulary

debate 278 argue (w/ myself) about
confrontation 279 face-to-face conflic
forte 279 strength; area of expertise
asset 279 valuable quality or skill
clunker 280 item w/ outdated technology
sought out 280 gone to see; looked for
sustaining 281 MM keeping up; continuing
emanating 281 flowing coming out
irreparable 281 unable to be fixe
ominous 282 threatening
quiver 282 MM slightest movement
cunning 282 ability to deceive; craftiness
emergence 283 arising; development
severity 284 seriousness

anatomy 284 body
savor 284 deeply enjoy
windpipe 285 trachea
array 285 well-organized quantity
pathetic 285 pitiful; worthy of contempt
defiance 286 refusing to admit defeat
sadistic 287 cruel for the sake of pleasure
futile 289 hopeless
staunch 289 stop (usually bleeding)
hypodermic needle 289 device to deliver medication under the skin
plunger 289 device to push material through a tube
exquisitely 289 intensely

Journal and Discussion Questions

1. List the ways that forming an alliance with Rue has helped Katniss.
2. How does Clove refer to Katniss? How does Thresh? What do you conclude?
3. Katniss takes bandages with her (p. 281). Why do you think she didn't use them?
4. Do you buy Katniss's saying she sang Rue to *sleep* instead of to *death*? Explain.
5. Summarize the chapter from Thresh's point of view.

Summary

Katniss re-camouflages the mouth of the cave with rocks and cleans her weapons. The recap shows no deaths, so Cato, Clove, Thresh, and Foxface may all come. The night is bitterly cold and Katniss keeps watch in the sleeping bag with Peeta. She accepts that it will be a bad night for herself, her mother, and Prim. She wonders if Gale is hoping for Peeta to live, what would happen if she were open to romance with Gale, and what Gale thinks of her kissing Peeta. She leaves for the feast three hours before dawn, with her supplies in Rue's small pack, making sure Peeta has water and the first-aid kit within reach, but putting his jacket over her own and kissing him goodbye as an afterthought.

Upon reaching Rue's copse, Katniss sees no other tributes, but doesn't know if any arrived before her. She figures that Foxface and Thresh may believe that Peeta is covering her. As the sun rises, the plain in front of her opens and a table emerges with four backpacks on it. District 12's is so tiny that anyone could take it along with their own. Immediately, Foxface slips out of the Cornucopia, snags her own backpack, and runs off. No one follows her. Katniss realizes she should have done that and must be next. As she runs, she hears Clove's first knife in the air and deflects it with her bow, shooting an arrow at Clove's heart, but hitting her upper left arm. Katniss reaches the table, shoves the tiny backpack up her arm, and is about to shoot Clove again, when Clove's thrown knife hits her forehead above her right eye, sending blood gushing down her face. Clove tackles her, pinning her to the ground and asks where Peeta is. Katniss says he's hunting Cato, and screams Peeta's name. Clove hits her in the windpipe, selects a knife from the array inside her jacket, and prepares to kill Katniss, saying that she'll die just like her ally, Rue. Katniss decides to die defiantl , but Clove is suddenly yanked away.

Katniss sits up to see Thresh hold Clove aloft, then fling her to the ground and demand whether Clove killed Rue. Clove denies it, but Thresh doesn't believe her. She yells for Cato, and Cato calls back, but Thresh bashes Clove's head with a rock, and turns to Katniss. Thresh demands what was meant about Rue being her ally. Katniss explains that she and Rue teamed up and blew up the supplies. She says she tried to save Rue, killed the boy who killed her, sang to her, and covered her in flowers after she died. She adds that District 11 sent her bread, and begs Thresh to kill her quickly. He says that he will let her go this once, for Rue's sake, and then they will be even. She agrees, and hearing Cato approaching, Thresh tells the "Fire Girl" to run, which she does, turning to see Thresh running off with both large backpacks and Cato kneeling beside Clove. She figures that Cato will go after Thresh and the District 2 backpack rather than follow her. Reaching the cave, she squeezes in, cuts open the backpack, grabs the syringe, and jabs Peeta's arm, injecting the medicine. A beautiful moth lands on her wrist, and—still bleeding from the wound in her forehead, she blacks out.

70   *The Hunger Games: A Teaching Guide*

Chapter 22

Feelings on Display; Haymitch's Feast.

Chapter 22
Page 290

Vocabulary

crave 290 long for; earnestly desire
tainted 290 spoiled; contaminated
haggard 290 exhausted
plaintively 294 sorrowfully
respite 294 a temporary reprieve
projection 295 image shown on a screen
sinister 295 evil and threatening
quicksand 295 water-saturated sand
irreverent 296 disrespectful
tirades 296 outbursts of condemnation

fabricated 296 made up; invented
reinforces 297 strengthens
prying 297 peering into other's business
evasively 298 to avoid revealing any more
lulling 299 soothing; quieting
exorbitant 299 unbelievably high (of cost)
riveting 299 able to hold intense attention
ramp up 300 rapidly increase
reluctance 301 unwillingness

Journal and Discussion Questions

1. Do you believe that Peeta's story about falling for Katniss is true? Explain.
2. What earlier incident does Peeta's father having loved Katniss's mother throw light on?
3. How does Peeta's response to the area where Thresh is hiding relate to his background?
4. Summarize the gifts Katniss has received and what she did to "earn" them.

Summary

Katniss awakens thinking she's at home, but finally realizes that she's in the cave with Peeta. The swelling in his leg is down, but Katniss is dizzy and weary. Peeta says it's his turn to take care of her. There is a storm, and rain drips through several holes in the ceiling. Peeta knows only that Clove is dead, so Katniss fills him in on many of the things she hasn't told him: allying with Rue, blowing up the food, her deafness, Rue's death, killing the boy from District 1, the gift of bread, Clove's death, and Thresh's pardon. Peeta is amazed that Thresh let her go so he wouldn't be in her debt, and Katniss likens it to her debt to Peeta for the bread and asks why he did it. He says she knows why, and when she shakes her head, he adds that Haymitch had said it would be hard to convince her, then changes the subject to Cato and Thresh, saying he hopes they'll finish each other off. Katniss suggests that at home they would have liked Thresh, and Peeta says they can hope that Cato kills him so they don't have to. Katniss is upset, but covers her emotions from the camera with Peeta's help and goes back to sleep.

In the evening, they divide the last of their food, deciding to hunt the next day. Katniss asks about the area that Thresh is in, and they discuss what they'd have to do to get a gift. Katniss, knowing that romance is the answer, teases Peeta about the resources it must have taken to get the sleeping syrup. But he is upset, saying the fact that they're both alive may make her think she did the right thing, and begging her not to die for him as it won't be to his benefit. She sees this as an opportunity to milk the sponsors and starts to say that maybe she did it for herself, but she stops before finishing the thought, saying (untruthfully) that Haymitch told her to avoid the topic. Peeta says he'll have to fill in the blanks, and kisses her, the first time that Katniss wants another. They both get into the sleeping bag, and Katniss takes the first watch.

The next day, rain impedes hunting. Katniss realizes that huddling in the cold won't get them gifts, and—given that she resents revealing her feelings—her best bet is to get Peeta talking. She asks when his crush on her started. He tells how his father pointed her out on the first day of school as the girl whose mother the baker wanted to marry before she ran off with a coal miner. Peeta had asked him why she would choose a miner, and his father replied that when the miner sang, even the birds stopped to listen. Then, in their assembly, Katniss sang, and the birds fell silent for her, too. When she finished Peeta says he knew she was the one, but he couldn't work up the courage to talk to her, so his name being drawn at the reaping was actually lucky. At first Katniss is happy, but she is confused by the fact that Peeta's story sounds like it's true and explains why he would have risked his mother's wrath to give her the bread. When she compliments his memory for detail, he responds that she was the one not paying attention. She says she is now, and when he says that there's not any competition "here," she does what she knows Haymitch wants and replies that he doesn't have much competition *anywhere*. They kiss until a thud outside startles them, and Peeta finds a silver parachute attached to a basket of delicious food, including lamb stew. Katniss imagines Haymitch confirming that intimacy is what he needs to move sponsors.

The Hunger Games: A Teaching Guide 71

Chapter 23

Thresh's Death; Foxface's Death

Vocabulary

withheld 305 did not provide; held back
repellent 306 repulsive
noncommittal 308 avoiding taking a stand
peevishly 308 in an irritated, annoyed way
depressing 310 dejecting; causing sadness
residual 310 leftover
authenticity 310 truth; reality
consumed 311 used up; spent
acquisition 311 collection of; getting of
extricating 312 freeing
preoccupation with 312 intense focus on
ego 315 sense of self-importance
outburst 317 sudden, strong emotional display

Journal and Discussion Questions

1. How is the word *murder* important in this chapter?
2. Is the moon Katniss sees in the arena real or not? Figure out if it could be by figuring how many days it has been since Katniss left home.
3. Why would Katniss's identity be a question if she won and returned home?
4. What does Katniss know that Peeta doesn't that allows her to work out before he does how Foxface died?
5. Summarize the novel thus far by telling what happened on each day.

Summary

They ration the stew to avoid getting sick, and return to their earlier conversation between servings. Katniss says if they make it back, it's unlikely his parents will want him liking a girl from the Seam. Peeta responds that in that case, she'll be a girl from the Victor's Village. Katniss realizes that their only neighbor will be Haymitch, and they make fun of him. Katniss reflects that Haymitch has been able to communicate with her through withholding, as well as giving, gifts. She asks Peeta how he thinks Haymitch won the Games, and they agree that he must have outsmarted the others. Katniss imagines that Haymitch started off trying to help tributes, but year after year watching them die became too hellish and led him to drink. She thinks he chose to get sober when he realized that this year they could actually win. She realizes that if she survives, she'll have to mentor future girl tributes from District 12 and is too repelled to consider it.

Katniss hears the anthem while serving more stew, but tells Peeta there can't be any deaths. But Peeta, looking out, tells her that Thresh is dead. At first she can't believe him, and then grows disturbed because while the audience, she thinks, could accept her sorrow for Rue, they won't for Thresh's "murder"—her first time giving death in the arena that name. Peeta points out that Cato will be hunting them again, and they hope that Thresh wounded him. Peeta wonders about Foxface, and Katniss predicts that she's fine. Peeta hopes Foxface and Cato will finish each other, and they realize that they'll have to be careful to stay awake during their watches. During Katniss's shift, she thinks about life in the Victor's Village and reaffirms her vow not to have children, who would not be safe from being reaped. She wonders how Peeta will change when they get home, characterizing him as a completely convincing liar, who has convinced all of Panem, and at moments, even Katniss, of his love. She decides that, in any case, they'll always be good friends who saved each other's lives. Her thoughts turn to Gale, and she interrupts them by waking Peeta, who pulls her in for a kiss. She says they're wasting hunting time, and they finish nearly all their food, saving just enough for a snack.

Leaving the cave, they feel their respite is over. Katniss gives Peeta the knife, noting that she has seven arrows left. Hunting with Peeta turns out to be impossible because he can't move noiselessly. Finally, Katniss shows him roots to dig and teaches him a bird whistle so he can confirm his safety, while she moves away to hunt, bagging two rabbits and a squirrel. As she heads back to meet him, he doesn't respond to her whistle. Panicked, she calls his name and almost shoots him when he appears out of the brush. Katniss's fear turns to anger, but Peeta, who has been picking berries by the stream, doesn't understand why she's so upset. She explains that with a whistle signal, it's essential to stay in range, and the situation recalls Rue's death for her. Then she sees that some of the cheese is gone and accuses him of eating it. He says he didn't and offers her some of the berries he has collected. Katniss examines them and recalls her father identifying them as nightlock, a berry with the power to kill before it even reaches the stomach. The cannon suddenly fires, and Katniss turns back to Peeta, afraid he's died from eating them, but he's alive and the hovercraft appears about 100 yards away. As she sees Foxface lifted from the arena, Peeta grabs her and urges her to climb as Cato will be upon them, but Katniss realizes that Foxface is Peeta's kill and shows him the berries.

72   *The Hunger Games: A Teaching Guide*

Strategy 20   Revising Hypotheses

Directions: First, read the information. Then, answer the question or questions.

On page 31 of this book (Strategy 5: Forming Hypotheses), I suggested the hypothesis, "Maybe Katniss's ability to understand other people's motivations will grow through trial and error as she goes through the experience of the Games," and you developed your own hypothesis as well. Since then, we've seen that forming hypotheses about motivation and behavior is actually a fundamental topic of the story itself. Each tribute has had to consider what the others might do; all the tributes who have formed alliances certainly thought about and formed hypotheses about the goals and motivations of their allies; and Katniss is continually trying to analyze Peeta's motivation for his behavior related to the star-crossed lovers angle.

It's always a good idea to revisit early hypotheses formed early in a reading in order to take into account additional details and information in the course of the story. Often, this may be signaled by an event or action that leads you to question your earlier hypothesis.

1. Given the evidence up to and including Chapter 23, is the hypothesis that maybe Katniss's ability to understand other people's motivations will grow through trial and error as she goes through the experience of the Games still viable? Explain your answer, identifying any evidence that supports it or calls it into question.

2. Write and review the hypothesis you created in Strategy 5. Write an analysis of its viability, providing evidence for your conclusions. If it is not viable, revise it. If it *is* viable, formulate another hypothesis about something different.

Chapter 24

Last Night in the Cave; Driven to the Lake

Vocabulary

outfoxed 320 outwitted a clever person
sustained 322 MM received; suffered
looming 322 hanging
considerably 323 by a large amount; a lot
drove to distraction 324 made crazy
unhinged 324 insane; crazy; out of control
enraged 324 extremely angry

finality 326 conclusion; the end of an era
deplete 326 seriously lessen; use up
rodents 327 mammals that gnaw
unearthly 329 seeming to belong to another realm rather than the earth
jagged 329 w/ an uneven, harsh quality
dissonant 329 being out of harmony

Journal and Discussion Questions

1. Do you find it believable that Peeta mistook the berries? Explain your answer.
2. Do you agree with Katniss's assessment of Foxface? Share the evidence you find
3. Why would the Gamemakers want the final fight in the open
4. Compare and contrast Katniss's response to the mockingjays in this chapter to her response when she was looking for Peeta.
5. What is the significance of the last word in the chapter?
6. Summarize the chapter from Peeta's point of view.

Summary

It takes Peeta awhile to understand Foxface and accept that she wouldn't have doubted the goodness of something they planned to eat themselves. Peeta says that it doesn't seem fair and apologizes for his mistake. He collects the berries to toss them, but Katniss says they might fool Cato, too, and puts them in a pouch. Peeta points out that Cato will know where they are if he saw the hovercraft. Katniss decides they should cook their food while they have the chance: the fire will show they're not hiding and their killing of Foxface will signal to Cato that Peeta's recovered. Given all that, she doesn't expect Cato to show up. Peeta lights a fire, and they cook, gather greens, and watch for Cato. With most of the food packed, Katniss wants to get into a tree deep in the woods for the night, but Peeta points out the impossibility of this with his leg. He asks about going back to the cave, and Katniss, realizing that he's asked very little and she hasn't been very nice to him, gives him a kiss and agrees. They walk back down the streambed but are exhausted by the time they arrive, and Peeta begins to fall asleep about halfway through dinner. Katniss tucks him in and kisses him on the forehead out of gratitude for his presence, not—this time—for the audience.

On watch, Katniss figures Cato's had it in for her since she got a better score than he did, and compares this with Peeta's graciousness. The recap shows Foxface, and Katniss thinks that she was the most intelligent of the tributes and Cato has neither her control nor her judgment. Katniss thinks about her own rage when she shot the apple out of the pig's mouth and considers using this as the basis for understanding Cato. Since her mind is alert, she allows Peeta to sleep till first light and then sleeps herself, waking to a hot afternoon. Figuring that today is the day that things will end, they plan to spend it hunting until the Gamemakers force their hand. Katniss lays out most of their food for a meal, while Peeta packs the gear. They leave the cave, this time for good, and going to the stream to wash up, find that it's bone dry. Peeta says the Gamemakers want to force them to the lake. Katniss suggests that maybe the ponds have some water, but they don't. Peeta suggests they go now, while they are rested and well-fed, and Katniss agrees. They embrace for a moment, and then set off for the showdown with Cato.

When they reach the plain, it's early evening, and Cato is not in sight. They cross to the lake and fill their water containers. Katniss says they don't want to fight him in the dark with only one pair of night-vision glasses, so they plan to wait for about a half hour and then take cover for the night. They sit by the lake, and—seeing mockingjays—Katniss sings them Rue's melody. Peeta observes that Katniss is like her father, and she tells him that it's Rue's song. Listening to the full mockingjay chorus of it, she hears how the overlapping renditions form an "unearthly" harmony. But something introduces dissonance, and the music changes into a shriek of alarm. Peeta and Katniss leap to their feet in time to see Cato crash through the trees, running towards them, but not holding a spear. Katniss's arrow hits him in the chest but simply falls aside, and she shouts that he's got body armor. Cato runs right past them, panting and sweating, fleeing something. Looking towards the woods, Katniss sees a creature come onto the plain and another six join it, causing her to immediately turn and run after Cato to save herself.

74 *The Hunger Games: A Teaching Guide*

Writer's Forum 8

Writing a Possible Ending

Directions: First, read the information. Then, answer the question or questions.

The end of a book needs your close attention because it usually is meant to tie up any loose ends, to put a final exclamation point on the themes, and to leave the characters in a situation of equilibrium, noting what has happened to all the important characters. The ending of a story should make sense of the foreshadowing and plot developments that have occurred so far in the book, and play out the main ideas that have been treated in the book so far. It should feel like the story is complete, unless the point of the ending is that the story is not complete, or unless the story is part of a series, which may continue with the same protagonist and antagonist, or shift ground.

Since this story *is* the first of a trilogy, we can expect that the conflict that will prove central to the second novel in the series will be revealed before this book is over. And since Katniss's has entered into several alliances already, it may be that we will have to expand our idea about the protagonist.

1. Write an ending for *The Hunger Games*, picking up after Chapter 24 ends on p. 330. Do not look ahead in the book as you do this. (Obviously, if you have read the story already or have seen any of the movies, this will be a different type of exercise for you. In this case, you will attempt to write an alternative ending that works.) Be sure to identify elements of the story that need to be settled because they've been foreshadowed, or because the plot has created an open question. For example, since the title of the second book is *Catching Fire*, we would expect that whatever the main conflict is will somehow relate to the fire imagery in this novel We would expect the Hunger Games to end and a victor to be declared and return to the Capitol from the arena. These are just a few of the items that should be addressed.

The Hunger Games: A Teaching Guide 75

Chapter 25
Page 331

Chapter 25

Muttations; Second Rule Change; More Berries; Victors

Vocabulary

attributes 331 qualities
hobbling 331 walking w/ a serious limp
hampered 332 hindered; interfered with
inadvertently 332 unintentionally
canine 333 member of the dog family
inlaid 333 decorated
dwindling 333 lessening

callously 334 w/out proper feeling
asphyxiation 336 suffocation
tourniquet 338 device to stop bleeding
vengeance 341 payback; retaliation
bound 341 leap
discarding 343 throwing away

Journal and Discussion Questions

1. Describe the muttations in your own words.
2. How is Katniss's killing of Cato different from her other kills?
3. Katniss reaches two deadlocks with Peeta (Chapter 20, 25) and one with Cato (Chapter 25). Compare and contrast the three, analyzing the situation, apparent choices, choice made, and the result.
4. Summarize the loose ends that you see in need of tying up.

Summary

Katniss is sure that the wolf-like creatures that stand on their hind legs and have flexible wrists are muttations. Cato has headed for the Cornucopia, and Katniss automatically follows him. Just as she grasps the tail, she remembers Peeta, spotting him 15 yards behind her. She shoots one of the mutts following him, but he waves her on, and she climbs, knowing she can protect both of them better from on top. Cato is lying on his side, catching his breath, but as she steps up to shoot him, Peeta—who has just reached the tail with the mutts on his heels—cries out. Hampered by his leg and the knife he holds, Peeta climbs, while Katniss shoots the mutts that are attacking him. Cato tries to ask if the mutts can climb, and noticing their distinct attributes, Katniss realizes the mutts have the eyes of the dead tributes. She screams, bringing Peeta to her side. She explains, and he gasps in recognition. The mutts begin a new assault, and one manages to grab Peeta, but Katniss grips his arm, and Peeta kills it. She hauls him back onto the Cornucopia and has just shot the mutt with Thresh's eyes, when she feels Peeta pulled away again. She turns to see that Cato has Peeta in a headlock and Peeta's calf is bleeding from a mutt bite. With only two more arrows, Katniss aims one at Cato's head, but Cato laughs and says if she shoots him, he'll take Peeta down with him. If she doesn't, she predicts Cato will heave Peeta's body at her. Peeta makes an *x* on the back of Cato's hand, Katniss shoots, and Cato understands too late. He releases Peeta, who falls against him and is about to go over the side, but Katniss grabs him, as Cato slips and falls to the ground. Peeta and Katniss embrace, waiting for the cannon before realizing there's not going to be a quick ending. After about an hour, the mutts drag Cato into the Cornucopia. Night falls, the air grows icy, and the recap plays, but Cato still lives. Since Peeta's leg is still bleeding, Katniss uses her shirt and her last arrow to make a tourniquet, hoping to save his life without endangering his leg. The next hours, listening to Cato moan and beg, are the worst of Katniss's life.

When the sun rises, Katniss sees that Peeta has very little time left. To put Cato out of his misery, Katniss takes the arrow out of the tourniquet and crawls to the lip, while Peeta supports her. She shoots Cato out of pity rather than vengeance. The cannon fires and the remaining muttations leave the arena. They move to the lake, and the hovercraft comes, but not the announcement of the winners. Katniss picks up an arrow to fix Peeta's tourniquet just as an announcement states that the rule change is revoked, and only one winner is allowed. Peeta says it isn't surprising and moves towards Katniss, pulling his knife from his belt. She loads her bow with the arrow, aiming at his heart. Peeta raises his eyebrows at her—the knife is already falling into the lake. Ashamed, she drops her bow, and they argue over who should die. Finally, Peeta rips off the bandage, and Katniss jumps to restore it, saying he can't kill himself. He says it's what he wants, and she says he's not going to leave her there alone. She knows that if he died, she'd never really leave the arena. Peeta says the Capitol has to have a victor, and it should be her, for his sake, but she catches onto the phrase "they have to have a victor," and turns it around—what would happen if there were no victor? She whispers to Peeta to trust her and shares out nightlock berries. Peeta kisses her and they stand back-to-back, their free hands clasped, count to three, and raise their hands to their mouths. As the berries pass their lips, the trumpets blare and a frantic Templesmith yells for them to stop and announces them as victors of the Seventy-fourth Hunger Games.

76   *The Hunger Games: A Teaching Guide*

Chapter 26

Recovery Period; Haymitch's Warning

Chapter 26
Page 346

Vocabulary

slumps 346 collapses
mangled 347 severely injured
feral 348 having reverted to a wild state
restraining 349 controlling
lag 350 delay
indeterminate 350 unclear
cadences 350 rhythms, pitch of a dialect
ecstatically 353 delightedly
enviously 353 wishing to own what someone else has
wallow 354 spend lots of time reviewing
compromise 354 agreement reached by all parties giving in
garish 354 crude; tasteless
contrived 355 artificial obviously planned
sophisticated 355 not naive or innocent
benign 355 harmless
musty 356 smelling of mold
orchestrated 358 planned and arranged
unraveled 359 made clear;

Journal and Discussion Questions

1. In light of the earlier uses of the word *rabid* (pp. 5, 295), explain its use here.
2. What does Haymitch mean when he says that Peeta "is already there"?
3. What are the five motivations Katniss offers for her behvior towards Peeta?
4. Summarize the chapter by telling how the new dangers are revealed to Katniss.

Summary

Katniss and Peeta spit out the berries, flush their mouths, and collapse in an embrace. The hovercraft arrives, and they are hauled up. As soon as the electric current no longer freezes them, Peeta falls to the floo, unconscious. Katniss sees the doctors preparing to operate on Peeta as a threat and pounds on the glass, screaming. When an injured person was brought home for her mother and Prim to heal, she could never understand why anyone would stay and watch. Now she is held by the force that held them: she has no choice. At the Training Center, Peeta is removed from the hovercraft, causing Katniss to hurl herself at the glass until she is jabbed from behind by a needle.

Katniss awakens alone in a doorless, windowless room. There are tubes in her right arm, she has been cleaned up, and the hearing in her left ear is restored. Trying to sit up, she finds that a restraining band across her waist. She panics, but the Avox she had recognized enters with a light meal, and sits her up so she can eat. Katniss asks if Peeta made it and gets a positive response and a hand squeeze that signals friendship. The effort it takes for her to finish the scant meal convinces her that she's been out for several days. She wants to see Peeta and Cinna, but she feels a cold liquid in her vein and loses consciousness. This happens several times before she awakens with no tubes or restraint and a duplicate of the outfit she wore into the arena for her to greet her team in. The wall opens for her, and stepping into the hall, she calls Peeta, but is answered by Effi. Her team is waiting, and Katniss runs to them, surprising herself by throwing herself into Haymitch's arms. She learns that her reunion with Peeta will be live at the victors' ceremony so it can be broadcast, and she is sent with Cinna to get ready.

Cinna and Katniss go to District 12's floo, where the prep team surrounds Katniss, and she gets her first real meal. The team then prepares her for Cinna, admiring her "full body polish." Katniss notices that all their talk about the Games is self-centered and stops listening in order not to hate them. Seeing the apparently plain yellow dress that Cinna brings out, Katniss thinks that he's given up on Girl on Fire, but in it, she appears bathed in candlelight. She notices the padding in the dress, but Cinna puts off her objections by saying that the Gamemakers wanted to alter her surgically, and the padding was a compromise. Katniss says she thought it would be more sophisticated, and Cinna "carefully" answers that he thought Peeta would like this better, which Katniss interprets as a veiled warning. Haymitch finds her and uncharacteristically asks her for a hug for luck. He holds her in place and quickly tells her she's in trouble because the double-suicide stunt made the Capitol a joke throughout Panem. Her only defense, he says, is that she was so madly in love that she wasn't responsible for her actions. He lets her go and as she straightens his bow tie, she asks if he told Peeta. Haymitch responds that he didn't have to because Peeta is "already there." Katniss realizes that her family, friends, and District 12 will all be punished if she can't sell her case. She sees that the Capitol will want to take credit for everything, and she must play along. She wonders if Haymitch's comment about Peeta meant that Peeta's already thinking strategically or Peeta's already that much in love. But she's having trouble figuring out her own motivation, let alone Peeta's, and wants to save these topics for when she gets home. For now, she has to face the most dangerous part of the Hunger Games.

The Hunger Games: A Teaching Guide 77

Strategy 21 — Interpreting Irony

Directions: First, read the information. Then, answer the question or questions.

Irony comes from a Greek word meaning "someone who hides under a false appearance." When irony is used, things appear different from, or even the opposite of, what they really are: unexpected events happen; what people say is not what they mean. Authors use irony to create interest, surprise, or an understanding with their readers that the characters do not share. There are three main types of irony used in this story.

Verbal irony is irony in the use of language. Verbal irony means that what is said is different from or the opposite of what is meant. It is often indicated by a conflict between the content and the tone of voice in which it is said. When Peeta says in Chapter 7, ". . . I'm sure the arena will be full of bags of flour for me to chuck at people," the rest of the paragraph, comparing his skill unfavorably with being able to wield a weapon is what (in addition to his general attitude expressed throughout) indicates that he does *not* believe that his skill is of any use. Verbal irony is not always sarcastic, but in this case, it is.

Verbal irony can also contribute to humor. When Katniss says (p. 96) after Peeta demonstrates his camouflaging skill, "If only you could frost someone to death," it is an example of verbal irony. This statements shows with wry humor how little application Katniss thinks this skill will have in the arena (which is itself ironic, because this ability likely saves Peeta's life—a case of situational irony).

Situational irony can occur either from the point of view of a character or the reader. It refers to either a) a situation when something that is expected with a great deal of certainty doesn't happen as expected (this can be from either point of view) or b) a situation when something that is intended fails to materialize (this is only possible from a character's point of view, except in Choose-Your-Own Adventures or other books in which the reader participates by making a choice). For example, Peeta's and Katniss's expectation that they will be declared winners after Cato is dead does not happen: instead, the rules are changed again.

In **dramatic irony**, there is knowledge that the narrator makes available to the reader, but the characters are unaware of it. With a first-person narrator, this is a special case because in order to do this, the author must have the narrator tell the audience about things that the narrator him- or herself doesn't understand and do it in such a way that the audience the audience *can* understand—but may not, if they miss the clues. This technique forms an important part of this book, as the audience is enabled to see beyond Katniss's unreliable interpretations and gather the truth about, for example, Peeta's motivations.

The inkling that the characters do not understand as much as you do or the suspicion that a character's words can be interpreted in multiple ways are signals that should encourage you to examine whether irony is taking place.

1. Keep a record of other examples of each of the three types of irony in this story as you review chapters already read and continue to read.
2. Is it ironic that this book has been made into a movie in which audiences watch tributes being killed in the arena?

Strategy 22 — Tracing the Hero's Journey

Directions: First, read the information. Then, answer the question or questions.

Mythology expert Joseph Campbell characterizes the hero's journey as having a set pattern on which a myriad of variations are played out. The hero leaves his ordinary life on a journey into a region where he confronts the supernatural. He wins a victory and returns to the world he left a changed person. Not every stage is present in every story.

1. Read each summary of a stage in the hero's journey to determine to what extent it characterizes Katniss's experience in *The Hunger Games*. Explain how each stage fits or doesn't

Departure

I. The Call to Adventure
The hero can enter into the adventure by mistake, or by being called by a herald who summons the hero. The call comes at a time when the hero is ready for inner growth. The hero's focus shifts from home to a distant place.

II. The Refusal of the Call
The hero is not always eager to assume the adventure offered. The hero has the opportunity to reject the call. If the hero refuses, his or her life may enter a state of paralysis until something happens to release him or her.

III. Supernatural Aid
The hero encounters a helper as the journey begins, a guide and protector (often an old woman or an old man) who provides special powers to keep the hero safe in his or her encounters with evil. This protector usually appears to one who has already accepted the call, but not always. In fairy tales, the helper is often a wizard, hermit, smith, or shepherd.

IV. The Crossing of the First Threshold
The hero, accompanied by the guide, goes beyond the boundaries of his or her everyday life, enters the wilderness, and has a first encounter with the dangerous forces of the unknown.

V. The Belly of the Whale
The hero is swallowed up by the unknown.

Initiation

VI. The Road of Trials
The hero undergoes a series of trials often on a perilous journey. The guide or other helpers support him. Each trial may bring new insight. Victories may be repeated, but are not lasting.

Return

VII. The Magic Flight
The hero's return to the world from which he or she came accompanied by his or her guardian.

VIII. The Crossing of the Return Threshold
The hero leaves the realm of the unknown and returns from the dark to the light. The transition is not easy.

IX. Master of the Two Worlds
The hero, through the journey, has won the ability to pass back and forth from one world to the other.

X. Freedom to Live
The hero can now live with new freedom as a result of the journey, having matured and grown.

The Hunger Games: A Teaching Guide

Strategy 23

Analyzing Diction and Style

Directions: First, read the information. Then, answer the question or questions.

Diction refers to word choice and patterns of word choices. It is an important part of an author's—and can be an important part of each character's—language style. Words, whether they are spoken or written, can be characterized along several ranges:

- formal to informal (this may partly depend on the context)
- current to archaic
- literal to figurative
- limited to extensive vocabulary
- originating in a single language to multi-lingual
- short to long, multi-syllabic word lengths
- standard to filled with neologisms (new words
- unexceptional to distinctive and idiosyncratic
- commonly known to highly specialized (e.g., the specialized language of a profession)

Other elements of a person's style include spelling, grammar, syntax, sentence length and complexity, use of punctuation, use of sources, tone, mistakes,, and idiosyncratic expressions. As you read dialogue in fiction note the elements of style and diction that, in addition to dialogue tags, help you to know who is speaking.

In some works, not a lot of effort is made to differentiate the way different characters speak, and the writer depends on the content and context rather than distinctive ways of speaking to differentiate characters' speech. This is how most speech in this book is differentiated.

Since Katniss is both the main character and the narrator, it is her style and diction that is most in evidence. But some conclusions can also be drawn about Collins's style and diction.

1. If a line of dialogue in *The Hunger Games* ends with the word *sweetheart*, who are the two characters who might have said it?
2. List some ways in which Katniss uses sentence fragments.
3. Which character mixes first person plural into her spee h, even when she is not with the others of whom she might be expected to say "we" or "us"?
4. Which character uses the name of the person being addressed the most?
5. Collins uses a very high number of multi-meaning words in more than one meaning. They are identified in the vocabulary lists for ea h chapter. Review the words and find them in the book What do you think of this aspect of her style?
6. In this novel, on p. 158 is a single sentence with alliteration: "Those who battled at the Cornucopia, with their superior strength and surplus of supplies, they couldn't possibly have been near enough to spot the flames then " On p. 315, there is a shorter reiteration of the phrase "spears and superior strength." What do you make of this as an aspect of Katniss's style?

80 *The Hunger Games: A Teaching Guide*

Chapter 27

Highlights; Exit Interview; Train Ride Home

Chapter 27
Page 360

Vocabulary

misguided 360 filled w/ wrong idea
keen 360 sharp
flaunted 360 defiantly made a show o
contraption 361 a mechanical device
berserk 361 wild; from Norse warriors (berserkers) who raged in battle like wild bears
ornate 361 elaborately decorated
unprepared 362 not ready
condensing 362 retelling in a shorter form
disproportionate 362 unfair; out of proportion
objectively 364 looked at w/out the lens of personal feeling
revive 364 bring back to life
instigator 364 person responsible for starting something
intoxicated 365 drunk
running interference 365 protecting from an encounter
insidious 365 treacherous; crafty
confining 365 holding captive
gauzy 366 like gauze; thin and translucent, allowing light to pass through
rapport 367 sympathetic and understanding relationship
plaques 370 tablets w/ an inscription to remember an achievement
alien 371 foreign; unaccustomed; strange
rebellious 372 defiant to ards authority
palpable 373 plainly heard

Journal and Discussion Questions

1. What does the fact that in the highlights, a "disproportionate" amount of time is spent showing Katniss and Peeta from the very beginning suggest to you? Explain.
2. Did your initial impression of President Snow change due to this encounter? Explain.
3. Why is Haymitch keeping Katniss and Peeta separate?
4. Why hasn't Haymitch told Peeta what he has told Katniss?
5. What has Katniss done that could have led Peeta to believe that —although she clearly wasn't interested in him at the beginning the way he was interested in her—her feelings had changed?
6. Why is Katniss's comment about the flowers eeta gives her ironic?
7. When Katniss says she is beginning to transform back into herself (p. 370), what does she mean?
8. What do you think will happen between Peeta and Katniss when they get home?
9. The genre of dystopias shows a dehumanized society as a means to address contemporary problems. Do you think it is justifiable to lassify *The Hunger Games* as a dystopia? If so, what do you think Collins is criticizing in our society?
10. Summarize the novel by either: a) drawing an image to represent each chapter or b) creating a title for each chapter to capture its contents.

Summary

The anthem plays and Caesar welcomes the audience. The victors' teams, and finall , the victors, are presented. Seeing Peeta for the first time since the Game , Katniss throws herself into his arms, and only when he staggers does she realize that he is holding a cane. They embrace and kiss and the audience goes wild. Finally, Haymitch shoves them towards a red love seat, which serves as the victors' chair. At a look from Haymitch, Katniss kicks off her sandals, tucks her feet to the side, and puts her head on Peeta's shoulder, while he puts his arm around her. The night's show—required viewing for everyone in Panem—is a three-hour highlights reel of the Games, which the fil - makers designed to tell a love story. Katniss gets to see how Peeta misled the Careers about her, that he stayed awake the entire night at the tracker jacker tree, fought with Cato to allow her to escape, and whispered her name in his sleep as he lay camouflaged in the riverbank. Katniss is featured as she holds Rue when she dies and searches for and finds Peeta and nurses him. The end is not the announcement of victory but Katniss pounding on the glass door, screaming for Peeta, which Katniss realizes can only help her story. The anthem plays again as President Snow takes the stage. What is apparently a single crown twists apart and becomes two, and the president crowns Peeta with a smile and Katniss with a glare that signals to Katniss that she is considered the instigator and the one to punish.

The Hunger Games: A Teaching Guide 81

Chapter 27, cont.

Following is the victory banquet at the president's mansion, where Katniss and Peeta are greeted by Capitol officials and sponsors, all the while holding hands. Back at the Training Center, Katniss hopes to speak with Peeta alone, but Haymitch sends him off with Portia and escorts Katniss to her room. Katniss gets up in the night and finds that her door is locked from the outside. She realizes the Capitol are responsible, sending her back to bed, where she only pretends to sleep. Cinna dresses Katniss in a white, gauzy dress and glowing makeup for the exit interview, which has no live audience. Caesar greets Katniss with a hug and strives to reassure her. Peeta and Katniss sit on the loveseat, and—at Caesar encouragement—Katniss snuggles up to Peeta as she had the night before. At first Katniss redirects the conversation to Peeta whenever she can. But then, Caesar tells Katniss that the real thrill for the audience was watching her fall for Peeta and asks when she realized she was in love. She hems and haws until Caesar says it hit him when she shouted Peeta's name from the tree, and she is able to pick up from there, saying that it was at that moment that she first knew that the romance might survive the Games. It is only in the interview that Katniss learns that Peeta has a new leg.

The critical moment occurs when Caesar asks Katniss about the berries, and she haltingly says that she couldn't bear the thought of living without Peeta. Peeta confirms that the same goes for him. Afterwards, Haymitch says she was perfect. Katniss collects the mockingjay pin, and they say a temporary farewell to their stylists, whom they'll see again soon for the victory tour of the districts. Then they are on the train, going home. Katniss washes off the makeup and puts her hair back in its usual braid, thinking of home and transforming back into herself, so that when she rejoins the others, Peeta's touch feels foreign. At a fuel stop, Peeta and Katniss walk down the track, and Peeta gives her flower , but they remind her of Gale, and thinking about Gale makes her feel like she's been lying to "two people." Peeta asks her what's wrong, but she doesn't tell him. Haymitch comes up and tells them to "keep it up" in the district until the cameras have gone. Peeta asks Katniss what this means and she explains that the Capitol didn't like the double-suicide since it seemed too rebellious, and Haymitch had been advising her so that she wouldn't make things worse. Peeta wonders why Katniss and not him, and Katniss tells him Haymitch knew he was smart enough to do everything right without being told. Peeta responds that he didn't know there was anything that needed to be gotten right, and asks if this means that everything in the arena and the last few days was part of a strategy that Haymitch and Katniss came up with. Katniss points out that she couldn't talk with Haymitch in the arena, but Peeta persists, suggesting that Katniss knew what Haymitch wanted her to do, and then asking her directly if it was all for the games. She replies "not all of it," but confesses that the closer they get to home, the more confused she becomes. In a voice filled with pain, he asks her to let him know when she works it out and walks away. The next time they meet, he only nods at her, and she feels he's not being fair because she can't explain about herself and Gale, since they've never discussed it, and it's hopeless anyway, since she's never going to marry. But she realizes telling him that she misses him already also wouldn't be fair.

As they approach the District 12 station, Peeta extends his hand to her, asking if they should keep up appearances for the audience, and she takes his hand and readies herself for the camera, fearing the moment when she will have to let him go.

82 *The Hunger Games: A Teaching Guide*

Strategy 24 — Rereading a Book

Directions: First, read the information. Then, answer the question or questions.

As we discussed in Strategy 2: Understanding the Reading Process and Strategy 17: Engaging with a Text Through Imaging, reading fiction is meant to be an experience. Novelist Joseph Conrad wrote, "My task, which I am trying to achieve, is, by the power of the written word, to make you hear, to make you feel—it is before all, to make you see. That, and no more, but it is everything."* In other words, we don't read literature just for the words that make up the story or to get at the facts; we read it in order to pass through (in our imaginations) the sequence of events the author proposes, allowing our minds and hearts to respond to these events.

But all of this doesn't happen without the extended and complex act that we call reading. And in our first reading of a text, we cannot give ourselves fully to experiencing the story because we have to perform all of the tasks that make up the reading process, from recognizing the symbols as letters and words, to figuring out the meaning of unfamiliar words, to recollecting the sequence of events, etc.

It is worth recalling what Vladimir Nabokov said:

"... one cannot read a book: one can only reread it.... When we read a book for the first time the very process of laboriously moving our eyes from left to right, line after line, page after page, this complicated physical work upon the book, the very process of learning in terms of space and time what the book is about, this stands between us and artistic appreciation.... In reading a book, we must have time to acquaint ourselves with it. We have no physical organ (as we have the eye in regard to a painting) that takes in the whole picture and then can enjoy its details. But at a second, or third, or fourth reading we do, in a sense, behave towards a book as we do towards a painting" (*Lectures on Literature*, New York: Harcourt Brace, 1982, p. 3).

Rereading is also important when we want to clarify, re-experience, or check on our understanding of links between different parts of a book.

1. Reread *The Hunger Games*. Keep track of things that you notice in your second reading that you bypassed without paying attention the first time. Write a brief compare and contrast essay, to show the similarities and differences in the two readings.

*(Preface to *The Nigger of the "Narcissus,"* Oxford: Oxford University Press, 1984, p. xlii)

Strategy 25 — Identifying Themes

Directions: First, read the information. Then, answer the question or questions.

The **theme** of a story might be thought of as the story's point or its message. A theme is often a generalization about life or human behavior or values—true, but not a truism—an author's insight into the way things work that he or she wants to share with readers. Through its theme, a story moves from the particular (a girl named Katniss; a group of teenagers forced to fight ea h other) to the universal.

Usually, theme is an important part of a story's meaning and is developed throughout the story. A short work, like an anecdote, or a story that is meant purely to amuse or entertain may not have a strong theme, but serious works may have multiple themes.

The message of a story is shaped by the author's intention and purpose. Besides patterns in the story (which often point to the theme), there are certain parts of a story that often refer to the theme: the title, the beginning, and the very end. An important character's first and final words are also likely to carry powerful indications of theme.

A persuasive or didactic piece of writing (such as a fable), on the other hand, might have an explicit moral—a clear statement of theme. Such a statement limits the interpretation of the piece. However, a piece of writing that was written with experience or aesthetic response in mind is more open to interpretation. Certainly the author may have a theme or themes in mind, but the readers bring their own insights and different readers may legitimately find somewhat different meanings based on patterns and messages in the text combined with their own interpretations and insights. We seek for a balance between what is in the text and what the reader brings to the text.

In a story, such as *The Hunger Games*, that deals with complex issues, there are likely to be multiple themes. But also try looking for a joining of the plots with a single, over-arching theme.

As you finish a book, before you turn to thinking about what you will read next, spending some time considering the themes can help you fix the experience of reading that particular book in your mind, since thematic analysis requires that you review the whole experience to determine what lasting meaning it might have for you.

1. In a dystopia, there are often two levels of understanding: the effects of the evils or ills being considered on the main character and the effects on the society as a whole. How does this work in *The Hunger Games*?
2. State the theme or themes you find as you finish reading the sto . Explain how you concluded that these statements are thematic, and include quotations from the story, as evidence of the themes you identified
3. Compare and contrast the theme(s) of *The Hunger Games* with the theme(s) of another "community" book or dystopia that you have read. How do you account for the differences (e.g., focus on different problems in society, different characters, different plot, etc.)

Writer's Forum 9

Composing a Book Review

Directions: First, read the information. Then, answer the question or questions.

In a **book review**, you identify the work you are considering by its title, author, and genre; briefly summarize the plot; and then state your evaluation of the work.

When you write the **summary**, it is standard practice to identify the main characters, including the protagonist and antagonist, if the story has them. You should also include basic plot information, including a brief description of the main conflict the setting, and the background of the situation, while avoiding spoilers that could ruin the reading experience for your audience.

Evaluation involves holding the book you're reviewing up to a set of preestablished criteria and then judging it based on those criteria. It requires much more than "I like it" or "I don't like it," although that kind of personal, gut-level reaction can form a part of an evaluation. But after that (or, perhaps, before that), it's time to become analytical and describe why and how the book in question succeeded in meeting or failed to meet your criteria. So your statements of judgment should include your general evaluation of the work as a whole (usually, book reviews are only written when a reader has finished a book) and show how your analysis of and reaction to elements of the work led you to that response.

For example, you might respond positively based on the following:
- The plot is suspenseful and interesting.
- The themes resonate with you.
- You like or admire one or more of the characters.
- The vivid description catches your imagination.
- The book is amusing and enjoyable.
- You learn something valuable.
- You are so absorbed that you can't wait to read more.
- You find insights or understandings that enri h your life.

Your evaluation need not only include favorable responses, however. You may judge the work unfavorably, if you think, for example, that the
- dialogue is unbelievable,
- characterization is weak,
- characters' motivations are not convincing,
- plot is convoluted or unbelievable,
- attitudes expressed seem inappropriate to you, and/or
- the genre doesn't appeal to you.

If your criteria don't match those stated above, you should clarify for yourself what you expect from the plot, themes, characters, language, dialogue, etc.

Sometimes readers change their minds about a work as they read, and it is also possible to write a review in which you explain how you began with one judgment and detail how and why your judgment changed.

1. Write a review of *The Hunger Games*. Identify the book, summarize the plot, and provide a criteria-based evaluation, supported with evidence from the book.

The Hunger Games: A Teaching Guide   85

Writer's Forum 10

Comparing Two Treatments

Directions: First, read the information. Then, answer the question or questions.

As you know from Writer's Forum 3: Comparing and Contrasting, in a compare and contrast essay, you show the similarities and differences between two people, things, ideas, approaches, etc., and draw some conclusion(s) based on this examination. You choose the categories to compare and contrast based on your purpose and your topic.

Sometimes you will want to compare and contrast multiple treatments of the same subject in different genres or media. You might want to do this if a work has been adapted or translated to create a new work, if a work has inspired or influenced another work, or if they have the same subject and enough in common or such wide differences that you think it would be fruitful to assess how the two treatments, with their similarities and differences, each make meaning and achieve their effects.

In this particular case, you are going to contrast the book edition of *The Hunger Games* with the live-action movie (2012). Usually it is easier to do this if you both read the book at least twice and watch the movie at least twice, once to experience it, and once to take notes for your paper. Here are some questions that would be useful to examine, citing evidence as appropriate:

- A movie has a limited amount of time, so a movie adaptation of a book generally leaves out material included in the book. What, if anything, is omitted or compressed in the movie? How did this affect the telling?
- A movie script may have additional material not included in the book, or may make changes in the book. What additions and/or changes do you notice? Did they add value? Did they make sense in the context?
- How did your imaginings of the characters, settings, and actions of the book differ from the way they were presented in the movie? Compare the characterizations and the plots carefully. Did the movie provide you with new insights into the plot or characters?
- Apart from the book, did the movie work as an experience in itself? Did it hold your interest? Was it worthwhile?
- Did the theme(s) you identified in the book come out in the movie? If not, what message(s) did the movie give?
- Which did you like better—the book or the movie? Why?

Source words that can help you express concepts of similarity and difference include the following:

- as well as
- similarly
- differ
- whereas
- however
- likewise
- alike
- while
- but
- on the contrary
- at the same time
- resemble
- conversely
- though
- on the other hand

1. Write an essay comparing and contrasting the book and movie of *The Hunger Games*.

Test: Chapters 19–27

Vocabulary

1. Analyze this group of words from *The Hunger Games*:

    abate   alleviate   deplete   diminishes   dwindling   quench

Put them in categories according to their meanings and explain your categories.

2. Look at each group of words. Tell why it is important in the story.

    a. strength, deadliness, cunning

    b. savor, windpipe, array, defianc

    c. melody, harmony, jagged, dissonant

Essay Topics

1. How are community connections essential to Katniss becoming a victor in the Games?

2. Who teaches Katniss things that are essential for her to know? Explain what each person you have identified tea hes her and why this is essential.

3. What is the role of music in this novel?

4. Early in the story, Katniss makes a point of saying she won't say thank you to Peeta because in the arena, in the context of a fight to the death it won't make sense. Who actually says *thank you* in the book and in what circumstances?

5. Compare the end of *The Hunger Games* to the end of *The Giver* or *The Lord of the Flies*.

6. What did Katniss think Peeta was going to do with the knife in Chapter 25? How does this event fit into the book at large

7. Why do you think the Capitol doesn't just let Katniss and Peeta die and skip a year of rewarding a winning district?

8. Does it make sense that President Snow is so disturbed by what Katniss did? Explain.

9. At what points does Katniss escape thinking as the Capitol would have her think?

10. Why is Part 3 called "The Victor" (singular)?

11. Explain in your own words how Katniss works out a way to have two victors.

The Hunger Games: A Teaching Guide   87

Theme Pages

Taste

1. The Latin proverb, "De gustibus non est disputandum" is often translated, "There's no accounting for taste," meaning that—in the world as we know it—taste can't be tied to other qualities such as intelligence, virtue, or good judgment. But taste *does* seem to be connected to other qualities in Panem. Discuss the distinctive tastes of citizens of the Capitol and what they seem to you to represent. Explain how you have reached your conclusions.

2. One of the facts of poverty—as experienced by many of the residents of the 12 Districts—is the inability to express their tastes through their attire, diet, and other choices. Because of this, the cases in which they can exercise their taste may stand out. Identify such cases in *The Hunger Games*.

Identity

1. Adolescence is a time of internal change and development during which teens build and discover their identities. In our world, this is played out through engaging in activities and making choices, and discovering one's gifts, talents, inclinations, and disinclinations. Yet teens have an audience in those they associate with: family, friends, peers, coworkers, etc. How does community affect the development of identity?

2. In Panem, a set of 24 adolescents in the Hunger Games are in a contrived situation, mainly with strangers, out of which (according to the standard rule) only one will emerge alive. In this situation, the preferences of the audience, who may become sponsors, can mean life or death. Explain how this situation does or doesn't change what you understand to be the underlying identity of Cato, Peeta, Thresh, Rue, and Katniss.

3. Do you think Katniss's status and reputation reflect the reality of who Katniss is? If so, explain how. If not, explain the gap(s) between who Katniss is and who others think she is. Be sure to specify whose opinion of Katniss you are considering.

Integrity

1. Peeta expresses the desire to die as himself (p. 141). *Integrity* might be a good choice of words to describe what he is hoping for. How would you define *integrity*? How does it relate to other virtues, for example, honesty?

2. Explain why you think these characters succeeded or didn't succeed in maintaining their integrity through the Hunger Games: Rue, Thresh, Peeta, Katniss, Cinna, Caesar Flickerman.

3. What advantage would it be to the Capitol if this quotation from Emerson were true? "In failing circumstances no man can be relied on to keep his integrity." Ralph Waldo Emerson

4. Explain the ways in which the Capitol's laws and practices are calculated to undermine integrity.

Theme Pages

Courage

1. Is courage the same as having no fear, or does it mean something else, and if so, what? How important is courage in your life? Do you need to do courageous things in your typical life at home and at school? Have you seen examples of courageous action in your community or is courage something that you tend to encounter more in books and movies and on the news?

2. Which major actions and choices in *The Hunger Games* do you consider courageous? Which one do you find most impressive

3. Consider the following minor actions and explain why you do or don't find them to be courageou . Haymitch's outcry at the reaping (p. 24); Cinna's advice to Katniss and Peeta to hold hands (p. 69); the filmmakers' hoice not to end the highlights reel after the victors are announced (p. 364).

4. Do you think the following quotation captures the idea of courage as it is presented in *The Hunger Games*? Explain your response.

   "Courage is rightly esteemed the first of human qualities because it is the quality which guarantees all others." —Sir Winston Churchill

Friendship and Loyalty

1. How do you define *friendship*? Which relationships in *The Hunger Games* do you think can best be characterized as friendships? Compare and contrast them and explain how they fit your definitio

2. What is loyalty? Which acts in the novel stand out to you as acts of loyalty? Are the acts of loyalty between friends or people with other relationships? Give names to any other relationships besides friendship that include loyalty.

Leadership and Government

1. What qualities do you think make a good government? Compare and contrast the government of Panem with your ideal government.

2. As far as we know, President Snow upholds the law, so what could one criticize about his leadership?

3. How do government and entertainment interrelate in Panem? In the United States?

Good and Evil

1. How do you define *good* and *evil*? In your experience are people generally one or the other, or do they have some admirable qualities and some less than admirable qualities? Explain.

2. In a fight to the death an individual is likely to see things in terms of black and white. In several cases, Katniss overcomes this way of viewing things. Identify when she does this and what the larger meaning is for the series, inasmuch as you can predict this.

3. Are there any choices in *The Hunger Games* that are clearly between good and evil, or are they more nuanced? Explain your response.

The Hunger Games: A Teaching Guide

Answer Pages

Strategy 1, Beginning a Book, pages 11–12

1. Answers will vary depending on students' prior experience.
2. Students may predict that the book will be about a some kind of sporting event, and may think that *hunger* is used figurativel . Those who have already seen the movie will have a pretty clear idea of the content.
3. Answers will vary based on edition. Possible response: A golden pin or brooch, formed from a circle with a bird grasping an arrow in its talons and centered over a black background. The entire brooch is on fir .
4. Number of years since 2008.
5. Answers will vary.
6. Possible response: Students' ability to interpret the title of Part I will depend on the meaning they assign to *tribute*, the most common of which is "to pay tribute," meaning "to praise." The title of Part II seems to refer to the Games in the book title. The title of Part III suggests that the Games have a single winner.
7. Possible observations: The language is colloquial and informal, with a number of sentence fragments, but also longer, more complex sentences. It's as if the narrator is reporting her whole life in present tense.
8. Possible observations: The narrator seems to be a teenage girl—practical, unsentimental, outdoorsy, responsible. She is telling all the details of what she does and thinks, but although the details are intimate, the telling of them is straightforward. Since she starts by telling how she tried to drown the cat, she doesn't seem like she's trying to hard to make a good impression or covering up—she seems to be honest.
9. The narrator, Prim, and her mother, are the only characters that have been mentioned: presumably they'll be important.
10. The story takes place in an imaginary world created by the author called District 12, an area with coal mines and a meadow, surrounded by a high fence with barbed wire on top, outside of which lie some woods.
11. Answers will vary.
12. Possible response: The coals mines and poverty suggest historical fiction set in Appalachia, but the name "District 12" and the "Hunger Games" suggest science fiction
13. Answers will vary. So far, the focus seems to be on staying alive in a poor area.
14. Answers will vary.

PART I THE TRIBUTES—Chapter 1, The Reaping, pages 13–14

1. Students who don't already know the story may believe that the story will be about Prim's experience in the Games and her return home (or not) and how her family survives her absence.
2. *Reaping* is a yearly ceremony in which a boy and a girl from each district are selected by lottery to compete in a fight to the death which everyone has to watch.
3. Answers may vary. Given Katniss's own cool, unromantic nature, as presented in Chapter 1, as well as her protectiveness of her little sister and her reserve with others, it may well be that the meaning is both figu rative and literal.
4. Their children are eligible for tesserae, which can help feed them, and once they turn 19, they are safe (although it may be unlikely that people would have children just to get their tesserae).
5. Answers will vary. Possible responses: The children are old enough that the fight might be interesting to an audience. They are old enough to be an integral part of their families and communities, so their deaths will be more heartbreaking and disruptive. Not taking adults means that the workforce is not impacted. Not being able to protect their children makes the district dwellers feel impotent and guilty.
6. Children of the Capitol, district children under 12, district adults over 18.
7. Answers will vary depending on where students live. Students may mention the (tyrannical) form of government, the (limited) education, the seeming lack of a right to vote, being fenced in, the poverty, the (lack of) employment opportunities.
8. Answers should include: trespassing; poaching; having weapons; thinking treasonous thoughts; blurting out her opinions when she was younger; making fun of Effie Trinket and the Capitol accent in the woods with Gale; selling illegal goods on the black market and elsewhere; her expressed disdain for the racketeers/informers; her description of the Hunger Games.
9. It seems as if the districts may not be adjacent—there may be large stretches of fenced off land in between them, keeping them separate.
10. Buzzards are known for eating roadkill and other dead animals—growing strong through others' misfortune. So the simile suggests that the Capitol is "feeding off" the deaths of the districts' children.
11. The key difference is that few, if any, of the people now living in Panem were even alive, let alone active in the earlier rebellion; they certainly weren't guilty of levying war against the government nor convicted with the testimony of two witnesses.

12. Answers should include putting out the goat cheese for Katniss to take hunting; waking up in the night and getting into bed with her mother; Buttercup joining her; arising for the day and finding Katniss gone (presumably to the woods); preparing for the reaping; Katniss's return; her admiration of Katniss dressed up; the untucked blouse exchange; the walk to the square; being segregated by age; and hearing her name.

Strategy 2, Understanding the Reading Process, pages 15–16

1. Answers will vary. Possible response: I read more slowly at the beginning of the chapter as I tried to get my bearings. I also read the history of Panem more slowly because there was some challenging vocabulary and because I wanted to make sure I understood the history behind the Games, which are the focus of the story.

Strategy 3, Marking a Text, page 17

1. Students' approaches to marking their text will vary. If you are distinguishing an aesthetic reading from an analytic reading, this should be saved for the analytic reading.

Strategy 4, Plot—Identifying the Overall Design of a Story, page 18

1. Answers will likely vary, but students may come up with something like the following:
   Act 1 = Part I; Inciting Incident = Prim being chosen; Reversal/Plot Point 1 = Peeta's declaration of love
   Act 2 = Part II; Conflicts = attempt to gain Hymitch's interest, perform in the tasks leading up to and in the arena; Reversal/Plot Point 2 = announcement that there can be two winners from the same district
   Act 3 = Part III; Climax = fight with Cato resolution is incomplete because this is not a standalone novel, but the first part in a trilog

   Exposition is a strong component in Chapter 8 (meeting Gale) and Chapter 20 (Prim's goat). Katniss's goal is first to stay alive; then to win for Rue and herself (Chapter 18); switches to keeping both herself and Peeta alive (Chapter 18); and shifts to winning the Games while breaking the rules (Chapter 25). In Chapter 26, it becomes to stay alive post-Hunger Game, preventing a complete resolution.

Strategy 5, Identifying the Narrator, page 19

These questions build on the initial questions about the narrator in Strategy 1.
1. Two. First-person point of view.
2. Answers will vary. Passages students choose should be in present tense, not past tense.
3. Name—We learn her first name when Gale greets her by her nickname and she explains why he calls her "Catnip" (p. 7); we learn her last name when she explains how many slips for the reaping have her name on them. Family members—We learn of her mother and sister in the first paragraph (p. 3) when she reaches for Prim and explains where she is; we learn about her father's death in her discussion of what he taught her about hunting (p. 5). Appearance—she describes her attire when she gets dressed (p. 4); we learn her coloring when she describes Gale and says she looks like him (p. 8). Age—We learn her age when she says how old she was when her father died and how long it's been since (p. 5). Location—we learn her location when she describes her trip from her house to the woods (p. 4).
4. Possible response: The narrator seems to say to the reader almost what she would say to herself, except that she wouldn't have to tell herself about herself. She is open about things that might be considered uncomfortable or embarrassing,
5. In addition to the observations from Strategy 1, question 8, she seems to have forethought (she doesn't plan to have children); be dedicated to and skilled in hunting; be resourceful; be a loner, except for her friendship with Gale and companionable silence with Madge; and she seems to be mature for her age, having been forced to grow up by the circumstances following her father's death.

Chapter 2, The Volunteer; the Boy with the Bread, pages 20–21

1. It adds to the emotional turmoil because the pick isn't final the child and his or her family may hope for a replacement and be agonizingly disappointed when no one steps in and therefore resent other community members, keeping the citizenry divided. It makes it possible for older teens who have trained for the arena (and who will put on a better show) to get into the Games even though they were not initially chosen.
2. Effie Trinket's way of speaking about the Games—both in the referenced speech and in her other remarks—shows her lack of understanding of the perspective of those to whom she is speaking: children are going to their deaths, but she sounds like she's hosting a TV game show. Her clinging to protocol in the face of Katniss volunteering seems callous, especially compared to the mayor's pained response. Her implication that Katniss volunteered not out of love but to prevent her sister from stealing all the glory is grotesque. Her desire for "promotion" to a "better district" (p. 28) shows her amorality and lack of understanding.

The Hunger Games: A Teaching Guide 91

3. Answers will vary. Possible response: "The strangled cry comes out of my throat, and my muscles begin to move again," (p. 22).
4. Katniss uses her history of interactions with the mayor to explain why he is pained by her going to the games, whereas to Effie Trinket, it's all "lovely."
5. Within seconds: her expressed desire not to cry (p. 23) shows that she is already considering the effects of her actions on sponsors.
6. Students' lists should include: Peacekeepers who are her customers; Gale, her hunting partner; traders at the Hob, with whom she barters, including Greasy Sae; the mayor, to whom she sells strawberries, Madge, with whom she keeps company; the entire District, who salute her; Peeta, who gave her bread when she and her family were starving.
7. She says she'll never know if Haymitch was addressing the audience or the Capitol in his outburst. Students may conclude that since he was "pointing directly into a camera," he is clearly addressing the Capitol. Others may think that he is addressing the people of Panem who, unlike Katniss, have not acted to protect their innocent children from the Capitol's Games.
8. Although the word is not used in the book so far, Mrs. Everdeen seems to have been suffering from severe depression. Her symptoms—lack of interest in usual activities; loss of energy; withdrawal; excessive fatigue; inability to act—are those of someone severely depressed. Students may cite websites like webmd.com or mayoclinic.com
9. In this paragraph, the narration seems like Katniss talking to a fellow resident of District 12. The question "Who hasn't seen . . . ?" presumes that the person being addressed has. The use of *you* suggests that her audience has or could have the experience she describes.
10. That Peeta burnt the bread on purpose is supported by 1) the fact that he had seen Katniss (and seen his mother sending her away) before the bread burnt; 2) by the facts that he only has one weal on his face and the words his mother says to him don't indicate that burning the bread is something he usually does; 3) by the fact that she has caught him watching her since; and possibly 4) by his reassuring squeeze of her hand, if that's what it was.
11. By the end of the chapter, Katniss has relegated Peeta to the role of someone who has to die for her to survive the Games.
12. Students should include the following: seeing Prim chosen, Katniss choosing to take her place, Gale taking Prim away, the salute, and Haymitch's outburst and fall; (students may posit that Peeta remembers the incident with the bread: if so, they should tell it from his point of view); Peeta being chosen, being afraid, but mounting the platform anyway; the reading of the Treaty of Treason; the handshake; and facing the crowd as the anthem is played.

Strategy 6, Interpreting Characterization, page 22

1. Characterizations of Peeta will depend on whether students believe he burnt the bread on purpose or not and squeezed Katniss's hand on purpose or had a muscle spasm. Possible response: Peeta is characterized in Chapter 2 as brave by the steadiness with which he climbs the stairs despite the fear in his eyes; generous and even noble by risking his mother's wrath and accepting punishment for burning the bread, and then further defying her by throwing the bread to Katniss instead of feeding it to the pig; devoted for his apparent continued interest in Katniss, as witnessed by the fact that she finds him looking at her and supportive for looking Katniss in the eye and squeezing her hand reassuringly. Prim is characterized in Chapter 2 as evoking innocence and youth, shown by her untucked blouse; her bravery is shown in her attempt to do what is expected of her when her name is chosen; and her love for and dependence on Katniss shown in words and her trying to prevent Katniss from replacing her.
2. The use of *gushes* and *trills* (p. 23) and *warbles* (p. 25) give the impression that she is "on" for the audience, completely oblivious to the horror that the chosen tributes are going to.
3. Peeta's mother's words to Katniss show that she feels superior to the poor people in the Seam and has no inclination to help them. Her screaming shows that she is shrewish, the weal on Peeta's cheek seems to indicate that she is violent, and her selfishness is shown by the fact that even when the bread is burnt she would rather that her pig had it than that Katniss did.
4. Katniss indicates that even though she feels that she is in Peeta's debt, she will not be thanking him, because thanks doesn't fit with the fact that they will be trying to kill ea h other. In contrast to Peeta, who looks her in the eye and squeezes her hand, Katniss has turned him off as a person, showing that she is in exactly the mindset that the Capitol hopes to create in its citizens.
5. Possible response: Katniss seems to be the protagonist, and—although she'll have to fight 23 other tributes, it's the Capitol that seems to be the antagonist.

Strategy 7, Plot—Foreshadowing and Flashback, page 23

1. Chapter 1 flashba ks: p. 3 Buttercup's adoption; p. 6 Katniss's former tendency to blurt out her opinions about the Capitol and learning to wear a mask; p. 8 her parents meeting; p. 13 entering her name for tesserae; p. 18 via the history of Panem being read; Chapter 2 flashba ks: p. 21 falling out of the blind; pp. 26–32 the context, content, and aftermath of Peeta giving her the bread when her family was starving.

Strategy 8, Analyzing Choices, pages 24–25

Answers may vary, based on students' understanding of the characters' motivations.

Choice	*Type*	*Motivation*	*Information*	*Extent*
Katniss's choice to volunteer for Prim	terrorized choice	Seeking life for Prim	Partial information; true as far as it goes; full awareness	Final
Peeta's choices that resulted in Katniss having bread	terrorized choice	Seeking life for Katniss	For burning the bread - partial information; true; fully aware; For throwing the bread, complete information; true; fully aware	Made in stages/ Final
Katniss's and Gale's choice to hunt, fish and gather	terrorized choice	Seeking life for families	Partial information; Aware; True	Repeated Final choices

Writer's Forum 1, Writing a News Story, page 26

1. Answers will vary, but the piece should meet the requirements.

Chapter 3, Goodbyes; the Trip to the Capitol Begins, pages 27–28

1. **Because she is going away**: telling them she loves them. **Because of her role**: Prim not taking tesserae and how to get by without, including Prim's goat and Mrs. Everdeen's apothecary business; trading with Gale for herbs for Mrs. Everdeen's apothecary business; and game; Mrs. Everdeen cannot allow herself to fall into another depression. **Because she doesn't expect to return**: that they must fight through what ever they see on the screen; that she loves them both.
2. The realities that are against Katniss winning the games are the fact that tributes from several wealthy districts have been trained their whole lives, and include boys who are two to three times Katniss's size and girls who are extremely skilled in knife killing.
3. Answers will vary. Students should show recognition that the education offered is state-controlled. As to what they need to know, understand, and be able to do, students may think that—given the Hunger Games—at least physical education, if not specific trainin , should be offered. They may suggest that learning about other districts would expand tributes' ability to understand the background of other tributes who they will face. They may go further and suggest that learning about other districts might plant seeds for connections between districts, hence the possibility of rebellion
4. The actual reason is likely to be largely related to Peeta's comment on p. 300 about his father wanting to marry Katniss's mother. Not knowing that, students may suggest (and this may be true as well) that years of trading with Katniss and a generous spirit that isn't just narrowly focused on his own family's well-being may prompt him to reach out to her, despite the fact that Peeta is also a tribute.
5. The details that make Madge seem very determined are that she comes "straight" to Katniss; that she seems neither sad nor "evasive"; that there is an "urgency" in the way she speaks; that Madge doesn't wait for an answer before pinning the brooch on Katniss's dress; that, beyond that, she asks Katniss to promise to wear it into the arena. Answers as to why will vary. Students may note that Madge is acting very differently than one would expect, given how Katniss characterized their relationship, which didn't seem to include much interaction. As a result, they may believe that the pin has a deep personal meaning to Madge or that it is symbolic of something.
6. Answers will vary. While most students are likely to agree that getting a knife and getting or making a bow would greatly improve her chances, they may strongly disagree that "it's just hunting" and that killing people can't be really different from killing game.
7. Katniss says she'll never know what Gale wanted her to remember.
8. Answers may vary, but many students are likely to suggest that Gale was starting to say, "I love you."
9. Katniss interprets the pin as being like a piece of her father that she can carry with her. Astute students may suggest that since the mockingjay was an unintended consequence of a failed Capitol project, that it may represent anti-Capitol interests or an underground.

The Hunger Games: A Teaching Guide

10. Students who have not realized that Katniss is an unreliable narrator or who do not have the skill to "read through" what she says will likely believe that Peeta is acting strategically to appear weak and frightened, even though this seems unlikely given his other traits. Students who have grasped Katniss's inability to read people are likely to suggest that Peeta is not interested in strategy and is not afraid to show his honest feelings. They may compare this to when he burnt the bread and gave it to Katniss, acting on what he felt, rather than acting strategically to further his own self-interest and avoid unpleasant consequences.
11. Students may think that *opulence* is appropriate to describe the rich furnishings of the Justice Building, the gold pin, the décor of the train, the fine clothes by the drawerful, and the food on the train.
12. Effie says that the tributes from District 12 in the previous year ate like "savages." Her choice of words shows Effie's shallowness, since to her, manners represent civilization, and the fact that she is taking children to a fight to the death is about the most uncivilized thing that can be imagined doesn't occur to her, making her statement highly ironic. In addition, her statement shows, as Katniss says, a complete lack of understanding of the situation in the district she represents, where children are starving and where simply having enough to eat would rank far above demonstrating table manners.
13. The phrase suggests that it is a planned part of a performance. Only students who have already read the entire book may realize that the same phrase is used on p. 341 of the muttations leaving the arena, which is, clearly, a planned part of their performance. The implication is that Haymitch fell off the stage on purpose. If this is the case, he may have done this to confirm that he was so drunk that he didn't know what he was doing, enabling him to get away with his attack on the audience/Capitol. Only students who have already read the entire book may suggest that Haymitch saw that Katniss was in danger of crying (p. 23) and acted strategically to draw attention away from her and allow her to regain her self control.
14. She points out that Haymitch is their mentor and, as such, their lifeline to sponsors and gifts, with the implication that his being drunk, rather than sober, may cost them their lives.
15. A Peacekeeper would have been aware of bringing the tributes from the stage to the Justice Building and leading Katniss to a room, while another Peacekeeper peeled off to lead Peeta to another room; the visits, in order, of Katniss's mother and sister, whom the Peacekeeper has to order out; Mr. Mellark, with a small parcel; Madge, who (perhaps) enters with a pin on her dress and exits without it; and Gale, who asks for, but is denied, more time, and has to be yanked away; and (presumably) escorting her to the station. (There is no indication that the Peacekeepers accompany them, so the summary will stop there.)

Strategy 9, Relating Setting and Mood, page 29

1. Students may interpret moods differently. Samples are provided for the first three chapters. You may wish to have students distinguish different areas in the arena, like the cave, the copse, in the tree with Rue, etc.

	Setting Description	Function(s) in Story	*Moods Created*
1	Everdeen home; woods; town square	reveals Katniss's homelife; shows how she stayed alive, despite extreme poverty; site of the reaping, which Katniss regrets being used for that purpose	bleak; hopeful; disturbing, terrifying
2	Town square	Katniss volunteers, sets trajectory for the rest of the book; Peeta is chosen, prompting flashback; Haymitch acts out	tense, inspiring, dire, heartwarming, humorous,
3	Justice Building, train	reveals aspects of Katniss's relationships to others and more of the characters of her visitors	grim, hopeful, surprising, heartbreaking
4	Train		
5	Remake Center; road to City Circle/Training Center (TC)		
6	TC: 12th floor, roof; woods flashback		
7	TC: 12th floor, training rooms		
8	TC: training rooms, 12th floor woods flashback		
9	TC: 12th floor stage in front of TC		
10	Stage in front of TC; TC: lobby, 12th floor, roof; hovercraft; arena Launch Room		
11–25	Arena		

	Setting Description	Function(s) in Story	Moods Created
26	Arena; hovercraft; TC: hospital; 12th floor under the stage		
27	Stage in front of TC; TC: 12th floor car to train station; train		

Chapter 4, Tributes Confront Haymitch; Arrival at the Capitol, page 30

1. Because the cookies land by a dandelion, throwing them out the window is able to serve as a segue to continue the story that Katniss began in Chapter 2 about being saved from starvation, which ended in just about when she spotted the dandelions while avoiding Peeta's gaze.
2. Students should mention Peeta's gift of bread, the realization—due to seeing the dandelion—of another way Katniss could access food; Mrs. Everdeen's apothecary book; Mr. Everdeen's additions to that book; Prim's help; the tesserae; trading at the Hob and in town to the butcher, baker, Head Peacekeeper, and mayor; and Mrs. Everdeen's herbal remedies. Astute students may mention Prim's goat.
3. Answers will vary. Students who believe that Haymitch acted on the stage to distract attention from Katniss and who believe he was attacking the Capitol in a clever way should mention those things, and may conclude that there is more to Haymitch than it seems to Katniss. Students who have thought beyond the book's narration may discuss the horrors he had to have gone through to be a victor and mentor every pair of tributes since, including, no doubt, children he knew, and offer that as explanation (if not excuse) for why he does not wish to be sober.
4. From Haymitch's comment, it seems that once he sees that Peeta and Katniss are going to play to win, meaning that his engagement with them and contributions to their efforts may not end in the heartbreak and horror it has for several decades of mentoring, he changes his attitude. This is supported by Katniss's revision of her view of Haymitch on p. 306.
5. Answers to motivation will vary, depending on students' ability to read Peeta through Katniss's unreliable narration.

Choice	Type	Motivation	Information	Extent
Peeta and Katniss do exactly what Haymitch says and don't interfere with his drinking or lose his help	terrorized choice (though Haymitch is not the one causing the terror)	Katniss: Seeking life for herself; Peeta: Seeking life for Katniss	Partial information; true as far as it goes; full awareness	Choice made in stages, every time Haymitch tells them to do something

6. Responses may include: Peeta and Gale; Haymitch and Effie Peeta and Katniss; Prim and Katniss; Mrs. Everdeen and Katniss. Foils later in the book include Cinna and the prep team; Cinna and Haymitch; Foxface and the other tributes; Rue and the other tributes, Thresh and the Careers.
7. Answers will vary. Students who do not grasp Katniss's unreliability may agree with her; those who understand her inability to read motivation and can "read through" her narration are likely to conclude that Katniss is misguided; Peeta's aim was, and continues to be, doing what is likely to save Katniss.
8. Having two tributes from a district, only one of whom can survive, sets members of each district at odds with each other. If there were only one tribute from a district, the whole district could unite around that person, and any kind of unity is undesirable to the tyrannical government because it could provide the foundation for rebellion. People who are at odds will not organize and work together.
9. Katniss's observations continue to make the tastes of people in the Capitol seem absurd and over-the-top (possibly *perverse*), but in contrast to the starving districts, they may even be labeled *obscene*.

Strategy 10, Forming Hypotheses, page 31

1. Answers will vary depending on the subject of the hypothesis, but should be grounded in the story.

Writer's Forum 2, Comparing and Contrasting, page 32

1. Possible response: Layout, architecture, sections or areas, government, security, employment opportunities, socioeconomic status of citizens, surroundings, relationship to other sections of Panem.
2. Students should use the applicable elements found in Strategy 6: Interpreting Characterization, p. 22 as their categories. The essay should reveal how strikingly different the two characters are in background, understanding, and style and reflect one of the two organization method . After students have finished reading, you may have them revise their essay based on the information revealed in Chapters 5–27.

Chapter 5, The Stylists Create a Girl on Fire, pages 33–34

1. Students should note: smooth, hairless skin, tattoos/stenciling, skin dye, hair dye, make-up, surgical alteration, youthful, sensationalist.
2. Flavius both says that Katniss looks almost like a human being and gives her the backhanded compliment of saying that having been prepped, she's not "horrible at all." The first is reminiscent of Effi Trinket's comment that last year's District 12 tributes were "savages"—it shows a complete lack of understanding of or interest in the situation in which Katniss lived before the games and an amazing ability to dissociate from the fact that he is helping prepare her to look good while dying as part of an entertainment. The second, especially given the adverb *encouragingly* shows an inability to shape his thoughts for his chosen audience. Katniss's response to Flavius's first comment plays right into his prejudices about the districts, showing her ability to do what he can't: adapt her words for a specific audience, in this one case.
3. It is degrading in that her grooming is taken out of her hands and she has to endure idiotic (even if well-intentioned) comments from her prep team. She is, as she implies, being made attractive in order to look good while being killed. On the other hand, given the terms of engagement, looking good can gain her sponsors and give her a shot at outliving the games, which she would not have without the styling.
4. In Chapter 3, Katniss's main focus is on communicating crucial information for her mother's and sister's survival without her, although she does tell them she loves them. In Chapter 5, apart from them—and both having interpreted the mockingjay pin as being like a piece of her father and being about to have her mother's braiding undone—she now wishes for a piece of her mother (and home) to hold onto.
5. Answers will vary depending on how astute students are. Katniss mistakenly believes that Cinna is assigned to District 12 because he is new. The fact that he asks for District 12 is suggestive; the fact that she doesn't explore this idea (although she certainly has other things on her mind) is also suggestive; and her collective misapprehensions about people add up to an unreliable narrator who can't read other people.
6. Like Madge, whose actions added up to something more than just a friendly gesture when she gave Katniss the pin, it seems that Cinna has some particular motivation. Later in the book, the fact that Cinna has the idea that Katniss and Peeta hold hands (which Haymitch later characterizes as a touch of rebellion (p. 79), and that he is the one that makes sure she has the mockingjay pin when she enters the arena (p. 145) support the idea that there is some desire to stand against the Capitol.
7. The meal allows Katniss to realize that even a dedicated effort at home would not allow her to prepare something comparable, casting further light on the disparities between the Capitol and the districts. It also puts her in extended conversation with someone other than Peeta and Haymitch, which allows us to see another side of Katniss, which doesn't come out with Peeta, because of her misreading of his motives and the fact of the Games, or Haymitch, because they're both somewhat acerbic.
8. Given that Katniss and Peeta will be fighting each other, students may find it surprising that any connection between them would be made. Some may counter that since they come from the same district, with the same product, that at this point, it makes sense to treat them as the District 12 tributes and dress them the same. Some students may point out the challenge of coming up with two different costumes for coal.
9. It is important for the sponsors to be able to connect the girl in the arena with the "girl on fire" in the chariot, as well as to follow the battle from her perspective and be encouraged to send her gifts.
10. Answers will vary. One possible response is that resources intended for Peeta can be redirected to Katniss if Haymitch can argue that that's what Peeta would have wanted, so that Katniss has a stronger chance of winning than with just the sponsors she can gain herself.
11. The crowd goes from chanting "District 12" to saying their first names, making it clear that they are gaining interest, and being seen as individuals, not just district representatives, which may mean that their support will cross district boundaries.
12. Answers will vary, but he seems neither impressive nor dangerous. The fact that he is small and thin could either mean that he is a figurehead with no real power, or that he is so powerful, he doesn't need to be an impressive person to wield it effectively.
13. Answers will vary. The comment is glib enough that it could be for show, and the narration cuts both ways by saying that his smile "seems so genuinely sweet"—which allows readers to emphasize the "genuinely" or the "seems," as they wish. Astute readers will see that the sum of Peeta's actions are interpretable as consistently genuine and not strategic (at least, not strategically aimed at Peeta winning).
14. She means that, she can act as strategically as (she believes) Peeta is.
15. Summaries should include: Cinna's waiting while the prep team prepares Katniss, his observation of Katniss's surprise at his appearance, his introduction, his sizing her up, Katniss's jump to the conclusion that he got District 12 because he is new, their lunch, his ability to read Katniss's disgust with the Capitol, his

96   *The Hunger Games: A Teaching Guide*

plans for her costume, his desire that she be recognizable, his weariness, lighting the capes and headdresses, and the idea for holding hands. (Presumably Cinna sees the rest onscreen, so he should be able to report on the cheers that switch from District 12 to Katniss's name, the roses, the kiss blowing, and the camera's fixation on the District 12 hariot, and Peeta's and Katniss's final ex hange.)

Strategy 11, Interpreting Name, pages 35

Latin	Trivial	Nature
Caesar - w/ a thick head of hair	*Flicker*(man) *-to flutter*	Rue - a flowe , herb; to feel regret
Titus - title character in Shakespeare's *Titus Andronicus*—he serves people for dinner	Glimmer - *a flicker of light*	Thresh - beat grain to separate it from straw
Cato - good judgment (ironic?)		
Clove - a nail		

Chapter 6, The Avox, page 36

1. *A* means "without"; *vox* means "voice": "without a voice."
2. First he covers for Katniss when she says that she knows the Avox. Delly is well chosen because she's so different from the Avox that Katniss knows he isn't making a real suggestion, but recognizes it as a chance to get herself out of the tricky situation. Second, when he and Katniss are on the roof, and she doesn't understand why anyone would leave the Capitol, Peeta understands why life in the Capitol is not ideal and blurts out that he would leave, but covers it by pretending that he meant he'd go home and not participate in the Games if he had that option.
3. Answers will vary depending on students' ability to read through Katniss's unreliable narration. Some may agree with her, while others will think that there is more to it than just distinguishing Katniss and Peeta from all the other tributes. Portia may have answered for a number of reasons: because Cinna hesitated (Katniss said he appeared weary when being congratulated, perhaps the reality is hitting him); because, Portia wanted to make sure that Cinna was properly credited; because she admired it; etc.
4. Katniss says (p. 82) that she doesn't know if the Avox saw her, even though she knows she did. She feels ashamed and guilty. Also, although she considered and decided there wasn't any harm in telling Peeta some of the facts, since he had covered for her, she doesn't trust him.
5. Katniss regrets not thanking Peeta for the bread (p. 32), that things weren't set right between her and her mother (p. 53), not holding on to her mother's clothes (p. 63), and not helping the Avox in the woods (p. 85).
6. The Avox would be aware of bringing in the cake to the group, who were conversing about interview costumes, Katniss blurting out that she knows her, and hurrying away; then being in Katniss's room collecting her chariot costume when Katniss enters and asks if she can take it back to Cinna, and departing.

Strategy 12, Understanding Symbolism and Motifs, page 37

1. Cookies, snares, rabbits, and coal aren't widely used story motifs and do not (yet) function as symbols).

Item	Motif	Symbol
fir	Prometheus myth	Peeta used fire to feed Katniss Girl on fir
Buttercup		a guardian; a survivor
Avoxes	Lavinia's tongue is chopped off in Shakespeare's *Titus Andronicus*	how the Capitol removes people's voices (e.g., no vote; tyranny)
the Hob		free enterprise; evading Capitol control
the woods	"Little Red Riding Hood" *Robin Hood*	"savior"
bread	OT Passover; NT the Last Supper	life
the fence		control of people by tyrannical government
cosmetics		unnatural; artificial contrast to nature
dandelions		hope; the ability to survive
mockingjay pin		rebellion; being out of the Capitol's control
the Hunger Games		the Capitol's control of the districts

Chapter 7, Training; Impressing the Gamemakers, pages 38–39

1. Possible response: Unlike the Justice Building and the train, which could be described as *elegant* and/or *opulent*, the shower is beyond anything anyone could possibly need, and—given Katniss's experience—seems to have features that are hard to imagine as desirable under any circumstances. The shower is better described by the word *decadent*: it seems to be a symptom of the desire for unrestrained indulgence, rather than a select (even generous) set of useful/enjoyable alternatives for the shower experience.
2. Day 1: Chapters 1–part of 4; Day 2: Chapters 4-6; Day 3: Part of Chapter 7; Day 4: Part of Chapter 7
3. Concealing their best skills leaves the other tributes in the dark about what to expect from them, giving them a strategic edge. Learning new skills adds to their repertoire, making them more likely to survive. Why he wants them to stay together is not clear, so answers are likely to vary on this point. Students may surmise it is to present them as a couple to the Gamemakers in the hopes that this will influenced the Gamemakers in some way.
4. Answers will vary. Students may believe that by saying that Katniss is a survivor and putting her chances above Peeta's Mrs. Mellark is alluding to how Katniss managed to survive at Peeta's expense when he threw her the bread. No other incident that could lead Mrs. Mellark to refer to Katniss particularly as a survivor has been mentioned, unless perhaps she is thinking of Katniss trading squirrels to her husband, but there is no proof, and there was an attempt to keep the squirrel trading from her.
5. Answers will vary. Some students may find Katniss's interpretations of Peeta's motivations a real stretch and think that Collins misjudged the believability of Katniss's twisting of Peeta's intentions. Other students may find it all believable.
6. Peeta may be referring to people's attachment to her, whether romantic (Peeta and Gale), or otherwise (other community members, Haymitch, Cinna, her prep team, etc.) or more generally to her charisma.
7. Answers will vary. The Gamemakers may have been impressed by the chariot costumes and want to see what develops; Katniss mentions what she and Peeta did well in a couple of training sessions without trying just before noting the Gamemakers' attention so the Gamemakers may be impressed with that; the Gamemakers may also have other ways of getting information (considering the tabs the government keeps on people), so perhaps they know to expect Katniss's archery skill.
8. Peeta couldn't disguise his hand-to-hand combat skills, and Katniss aced the edible plants test.
9. Answers will vary. Rue might be scouting them for an alliance; just as Katniss connects her with Prim, Rue might connect Katniss with someone she loves; though it seems unlikely, she might be spying.
10. Students' clarity on this point will depend on their ability to "read through" Katniss's analysis of Peeta's motivation. Possible responses 1) They're both pretending in order to make Haymitch keep his promise: Peeta's nicer about it than Katniss is, but it's all a sham. 2) It's clear that they don't. Katniss thinks that it is a sham, a strategic ploy for the Games and doesn't want to "pretend" when no one else sees them (p. 100). Astute students may note that what Katniss perceives as Peeta's "tired" response (p. 100) is reminiscent of her comment about Cinna being weary (p. 67): tiredness seems to be her go-to attribution for people whose emotions she is unable to parse. A better explanation is that Peeta is in love with her, knows very well that she's not in love with him, but intends to help save her life and is hurt by her misreading of his motives as well as traumatized by the fact that she might die.
11. Answers will vary. Students may predict that they will give her a zero as punishment; that they will give her moderate credit for shooting well; or that they will focus on her talent rather than her violation of protocol and reward her for an excellent shot.
12. On the first day, they are the last to arrive, and Atala gives them instructions. They spend time tying knots and working on camouflage. Katniss notices the Gamemakers fixating on them. It is not clear on what days they worked on starting fire, knife throwing, making shelters, or hand-to-hand combat. It is also not clear when the conversation about the breads and the bear happened. On the second day, Rue follows them and joins them in stations having to do with climbing, plants, and hitting a target with a slingshot. The third day of training, after lunch, is when demonstrations for the Gamemakers take place.

Chapter 8, The Scoring; How Katniss and Gale Met, page 40

1. It could reflect Katniss's realization of how the Gamemakers' perceived the arrow flying toward them and allows Collins to play out the reaction from Katniss's team, who leap to faulty conclusions (pp. 102, 103, 106). But would Katniss give her team the impression that she attacked the Gamemakers, and repeat it over and over? It may seem more likely that she'd state her intention (to distract them from the pig) and her success (she nailed the apple), along with her concerns about walking out unbidden. Students may conclude that Collins has Katniss speak out of character to create a plot point. In the movie, the line is given

to President Snow, which makes more sense.
2. Peeta gives her food that sustains her as soon as he realizes that she needs it and when she and her family are in dire straits. He inadvertently triggers her realization that she can get food for herself in ways that she hadn't considered. Gale becomes Katniss's partner, trades skills and tools with her, partners with her in trading the food they get, and helps her obtain food on an ongoing basis.
3. Possible responses: 1) Peeta really is the strategic player that Katniss has (nearly) always taken him for, and he now believes that separate coaching will improve his chances of surviving; 2) Peeta is planning to use his interview to help Katniss because he loves her, but realizes that since she thinks he's faking, she'll ruin it if she knows. With separate coaching, he'll be able to pull it off despite her; 3) Peeta is so hurt by Katniss's lack of trust that he is withdrawing to protect himself. After reading further, students may conclude that the strategy of teaming up with the Careers was evolved in the separate coaching sessions.
4. The line graph should show Katniss's emotional ups and downs in the chapter.

Strategy 13, Understanding Character Traits as Ranges, page 41

1. Answers will vary. Possible responses may include the following details:

honest/deceptive: Katniss is purposefully deceptive in engaging in the "strategic" romance with Peeta, although she begins to feel something for him—she's not sure what—during the Games. She lies to Peeta about the Avox out of shame and guilt, she lies about Peeta's health after she finds him in order to spare him, and she lies about going to the feast at the Cornucopia in order to save his life. Peeta lies when he says his interview declaration of love is a bluff to avoid antagonizing/hurting Katniss; he lies to the Careers in order to prevent them from killing Katniss; and he lies about the state of his health (and accepts some of Katniss's lies) in order to avoid worrying Katniss. Being deceptive is part of the Gamemakers' jobs: they are "honest" in that many things in the arena have the effects that they can be expected to have in the real world: nightlock berries kill you; water quenches your thirst. But they are deceptive in having rigged and booby-trapped the arena, and created many artificial danger .

self-serving/generous: Katniss is motivated to "really try" to win the Games by her promise to Prim—and this promise (along with the terrorism of the Capitol) shapes her choices thereafter. Beyond that, we can say that she is self-serving in that she teams up with Peeta when the rules change partly to avoid being a pariah and comes up with the berry ploy in order to avoid the horror she believes she would experience forever after if Peeta died and she lived. On the generous side, she volunteered as tribute to save Prim, she trusts Rue enough to share a sleeping bag with her, rush to her aid knowing it might be an ambush, and cover her with flower , risking the Capitol's wrath. Given that students accept that Peeta is really in love with Katniss, he is uniformly generous, and does not ever seem to act in a self-serving way. The most he can be accused of is eating ahead of schedule in the cave. Haymitch's withdrawal and use of liquor is self-serving but needs to be contextualized with the fact that it allows him to bear to be alive with his memories of the Games and the tributes he mentored and lost. It is hard to find anything wrong with his coa hing of Katniss and Peeta. Even when he is hard on Katniss, it is in the interest of her winning the Games.

insightful/misguided: Katniss manages to suss out Flavius, but is often wrong in reading people, including Gale, Haymitch, Peeta, and Cinna (all of whom love her in various ways), and their motivations. As a result, she often acts in ways that are misguided. Haymitch is insightful enough to get two tributes out of the stadium alive. This adds weight to the argument that his actions on the reaping stage were carefully planned and done for strategic impact. Peeta is very savvy at reading people and at thinking on his feet and responding in contextually appropriate ways. He reads Katniss far better than she reads him and is able to correct for both her faux pas and his own (Chapter 6). Rue is able to discern that Katniss is trustworthy and that Peeta really loves Katniss (is not acting). That she stays alive as long as she does suggests that she does not make many (if any) wrong judgments. Gale is misguided in attacking Madge and comparing killing humans to killing game, although his other strategic advice to Katniss is sound.

responsible/irresponsible: Katniss primarily acts responsibly by her lights. Even in blowing up the supplies and going to the feast at the Cornucopia, she tries to take precautions. But since her lights aren't always that bright, and since she acts out her frustration physically, she hits the irresponsible end of the scale pretty hard, for example, pushing Peeta into the urn. It's hard to find anything irresponsible to tag eeta with. Students who don't understand his motivation, however, may find his insistence that Katniss not go to the feast or he will crawl after her and his pulling off his bandage upon the second rule change irresponsible. Haymitch's irresponsibility in being drunk when he should have been mentoring may be put down to the number of reapings and train rides he's shared with tributes who are now dead. From the point of his deal with Katniss and Peeta, he seems to remain functional and do everything he can to help them, even if Katniss doesn't always understand his actions.

The Hunger Games: A Teaching Guide 99

2. Answers will vary, depending on the character chosen. Students should base their conclusions on a wide variety of the ways in which character is revealed, which they learned about in Strategy 6: Interpreting Character, p. 22.
3. Over the course of the book, Katniss partners with Gale, with her team, with Peeta, with Rue, and—in a special way through the gifts—with Haymitch. With Gale, she takes on multiple roles, as they both focus on gaining food; with Peeta, her relationship is never honest because it all takes place in the context of trying to stay alive in the Games, so it's unclear what the relationship is; with Rue—partly because Katniss is the stronger party and because Rue reminds her of Prim—there is absolute trust and love: it's hard to know what would have happened had Rue not been killed; her partnership with Haymitch is one of two distrustful, irritable people who can read each other (though Haymitch knows a lot that Katniss isn't aware she doesn't know).

Chapter 9, The Interviews, pages 42–43

1. None. Peeta keeps showing evidence of valuing Katniss highly and being worthy of her trust. She has some sense of this, but keeps denying it because her only way of interpreting the Games is that the Games inevitably must undermine any trust or feeling between tributes, even though Peeta doesn't seem to be acting on this premise: he is not behaving like someone who is planning on killing her if he gets the chance. She is terrible at reading his motivation, and she may partly be upset because she didn't see the change coming.
2. Answers will vary. Most students may not think that Peeta shows the kind of competitiveness that Katniss attributes to him.
3. Effie compares her frustration with Katniss to Katniss's abhorrence of an audience who is betting on her life: they are not comparable.
4. Katniss feels that giving any crumb of herself or any goodwill to the audience of the interview is a violation. Haymitch doesn't insist that she tell the truth—he suggests that she lie—but he sees it as an opportunity to save her life that she is throwing away.
5. While Peeta has a style that he can carry over to the interview, Katniss cannot, even with Haymitch's help, identify a style that works for her: she cannot identify who she is. Her father said that she'll survive as long as she could find herself (meaning the Katniss plant) but she is in danger of not winning any sponsors, hence, not surviving in the arena, if she cannot find herself in the sense of presenting herself in the interview. By saying she is "no one at all" (p. 118), she makes a strong connection with her father's words.
6. In both cases, Katniss is acting out, but in different ways. And while she can see the Avox's actions as helpful, she cannot interpret Haymitch's actions in that way.
7. Haymitch said that Katniss has spunk, which is a synonym of *spirit*. It seems very likely that they see similar things, given that strength of spirit is one of Katniss's strongest traits, if not the strongest.
8. Unlike Haymitch and Effie Trinket—whom Katniss treats as part of the Games establishment—and despite his role in the Games, Katniss is able to treat Cinna as a friend.
9. Answers may vary. Some students may say that it seems that Katniss was taking out her hatred of the Games on Haymitch. Haymitch only told Katniss the truth about how she appears, and he tried really hard to provide her with a variety of ways to approach the interview (and didn't start drinking until around *witty*, which probably showed enormous self-restraint). Others may say that Haymitch should have sugar-coated his criticisms, given who he was dealing with, and that he was unnecessarily harsh.
10. Answers will vary. Some students may not make the connection between Katniss's behavior and the separate coaching. Other students will believe that Haymitch and Peeta planned Peeta's approach to help Katniss but couldn't let Katniss in on it because—as became clear by her behavior with Haymitch in Chapter 9—she can't act or disguise her feelings.
11. Answers will vary, partly depending on whether students accept Katniss's assessment that Caesar does his best for the tributes. Obviously, most of the people he interviews die within a few days. He may feel that he gives them the best possible chance, given the system.
12. Answers will vary. Students may not realize that Peeta's declaration is genuine nor that it was couched as it was in order to provide maximum benefit to Katnis , in which case, they may think that Peeta is acting strategically to try to garner attention and sponsors for himself.
13. In the summary in which Peeta is being strategic, students should make it clear that he wants to be on his own in order to serve his own ends (staying alive) without having to deal with Katniss any more than he has to. In this version, saying he is in love with her is using her in the most grotesque possible way: making himself look interesting at her expense. In the summary in which Peeta is honest, he loves Katniss and wants others to see her as lovable, which she has a major challenge conveying herself. By declaring his love in these circumstances, he hopes to convince sponsors to see her as he does.

Strategy 14, Identifying References, Allusions, and Parody, page 44

1. Collins takes on the elaborate preparation that goes into "reality," the cutting and doctoring of what the audience sees, the interference from the show's producers in the storyline, and the spin put on things in the broadcast.

Test, Chapters 1–9, page 45

Vocabulary

1. Effie Trinket uses both these words to refer to District 12 residents.
2. These words have to do with Katniss's illegal activities in the woods of District 12.
3. These words describe aspects of the reaping.
4. These words have to do with Haymitch's outburst and fall off the stage at the District 12 reaping.
5. These words have to do with the Capitol's genetic engineering program and its aftermath.
6. These words have to do with Katniss's performance for the Gamemakers on the third training day.
7. These words have to do with Katniss's, Rue's, and Peeta's interviews.

Essay Topics

1. While there are no gods or religions in Panem (possibly because the authority of a religious hierarchy would take away from the authority of the Capitol), nature is closely related to some things that religion often supplies. Many characters names, instead of being revered saints, come from nature. Instead of religious texts providing the metaphors for deep-seated feelings, nature does. Instead of a savior god, nature is savior. Nature "creates" the mockingjay out of the Capitol's jabberjay, bringing good out of evil.
2. In Katniss's favor are her skill as a hunter, gatherer, fishe , and archer, her knowledge of edible plants, her determination and spirit, and her connections with a variety of people. Her ability to admit when she's wrong (as shown in her attempt to apologize to the Avox) is also in her favor, as is her support team.
3. Answers will vary. Students may find the pun too silly for Katnis , and out of character: she is not one to frequently indulge in word play.
4. Students may argue that the tastes of those in the Capitol (such as orange corkscrew curls and pea green skin) are each person's choice to make as they wish, but it seems clear that Collins is trying to present the Capitol residents as making choices and living a lifestyle that is offensive in its wastefulness and self-indulgence; obscene when compared to the lifestyle (and starvation) in the districts, and morally bankrupt, in the case of watching the Games as entertainment.
5. Answers will vary. Suggestions should be in keeping with the novel so far.
6. Answers will vary. Possible response: Having said that she felt betrayed by Peeta and that Haymitch is destructive, and given her limited ability to interpret other people's motivation, it doesn't seem likely that Katniss will appreciate how it will work in her favor.
7. Answers will vary. Students may suggest that Collins got carried away with the image of Katniss sitting up, swinging her legs over the edge of the bed, and sliding into her boots in one motion, and may not have really thought out the practical implications.
8. Some students may take this to be a case of mutual misunderstanding and objectification Others may think that Collins intended a difference: that Katniss's appearance is natural, and the Capitol residents' appearances are meant to reveal excess and demonstrate poor judgment, so Flavius's inability to see Katniss's humanity is a failing due to his removal from real life and Katniss's inability to see Flavius's humanity is because he has sacrificed his humanity to a certain degre , to become a work of art (or a wannabe work of art).
9. Some students may think that since Katniss gave the audience what it wanted, she still behaved like a trained dog, even if she did it by talking with Cinna instead of some other ploy or approach. They may point out that Katniss herself, however, doesn't seem aware of this. Others may feel that Katniss, with Cinna's help, found a way to do the interview on her own terms, and that's really all she was looking for.

PART II THE GAMES—Chapter 10, "An Object of Love"; "To Die as Myself," pages 46–47

1. Answers will vary. On the one hand, students may point out what a bad actor Katniss is and what a poor judge of others' feelings and motivations, surmising that she would have a difficult time telling if someone else were acting. On the other hand, they may feel from what Casar says in the interviews we hear that he does really connect to the tributes and feel for them.
2. She means that she "knows" that the entire love story is a fraud so that for Peeta to say he's in love with her is just to make himself look sympathetic to gain sponsors at her expense.
3. Answers will vary but should suggest something that Haymitch would be capable of doing. Some students may suggest that the dramatic unfolding of Peeta's revelation may have been developed with Haymitch.

The Hunger Games: A Teaching Guide 101

Others may suggest that after his questions about Gale, Peeta wouldn't want to take things any further, but Haymitch convinced him that it was in Katniss's best interest for the "unrequited love story" to be highlighted.
4. The allusion is to Shakespeare's play *Romeo and Juliet* (I, i, 5–6):

    "From forth the fatal loins of these two foes, / A pair of star-cross'd lovers take their life."

    It has become a trope (a widely used literary device) and refers to lovers who are doomed. In the context of *The Hunger Games* it means that Peeta's love for Katniss has no chance because at least one of them, and possibly both, will die in the arena.
5. Students who believe Peeta is truly in love with Katniss may see this differently than those who don't. If it were all strategy (no real feelings), then she would have an argument that she should have been told. However, since a) it wasn't and b) Katniss can't act (literally) to save her life, her reaction was much better (read, more likely to win sponsors) with it coming as a surprise.
6. Answers will vary. Students may conclude that Peeta has given up trying to convince Katniss that he really loves her; that he thinks that it's better to allow her to believe her conviction that it's all strategic is true for the sake of harmony and/or effectiveness; that he is being a gentleman, since he has gathered that she is actually interested in Gale and—while he went ahead with the act in order to make Katniss appear lovable—he wants to avoid making things any harder for her than they already are.
7. When a tribute is on-camera, s/he can demonstrate capabilities and an admirable attitude. A tribute can also speak directly to sponsors and mentors (though without knowing if they will hear it).
8. It reveals that, even with Katniss and Peeta, Effie does not consider District 12 a "decent" district, and she is more concerned about her career arc than she is about their staying alive.
9. Her identity—which was at issue in Chapter 9—continues to be an important question, as in the arena, who she is to the audience may be more important than who she is (in reality, to herself).
10. The first use of *silhouette* refers to a target to be attacked. As he prepares to enter the arena, Collins presents Peeta as appearing like a target, symbolizing the dehumanizing effect of the Games.
11. He wants to maintain his values and integrity and not let his actions be ruled by the context of the Games. Students may point out that this is similar to what Katniss says in Chapter 9 about being a trained dog and think that, given this, she ought to understand what he means.
12. Possible responses: A tribute could try to just hide out, avoiding contact, outlast the others without participation; alternatively he or she could commit suicide, either through his/her own actions or by not fighting back when encountering other tributes, or by allowing one of the Gamemakers attacks to kill him or her.
13. Students may suggest that even the Capitol residents have limits on their definition of entertainment
14. The catacombs are a subterranean cemetery in Rome where it is believed that persecuted Christians went to bury their dead in secret. A number of martyrs are also buried there, and therein may lie the connection.
15. The Capitol prefers to use euphemisms to cover the real meaning of places and rituals associated with the deadly Hunger Games, while the districts use metaphors that capture their horror.
16. Students may find it extremely unlikely that a pin with an emblem that if nothing else, commemorates the failure of a Capitol scheme (the jabberjays) would be allowed.
17. The smell of pine trees signals a wood (familiar territory) and wood for making fire and potentially, a bow.
18. Cinna is present at the end of Peeta's interview, the aftermath of Katniss shoving Peeta, dinner, and possibly Effies and Haymitch's final word . In the morning, he brings her a shift, escorts her to the hovercraft, where the tracker is inserted, and helps her prepare and keeps her company in the Launch Room.

Chapter 11, The Games Begin; Search for Water; Peeta Joins Careers, page 48

1. The death of the District 9 boy so early likely stunned and horrified resident , who will be angry with District 2 for killing him and Katniss for distracting his attention, leading to his death. District 2 residents will be proud of their girl's prowess with a knife and wish she'd succeeded in killing Katniss. District 12 residents will be relieved that Katniss escaped. And Capitol residents will react depending on which tribute(s) they bet on.
2. Through disobeying, she gains the square of plastic, the backpack, a reflective sleeping ba , crackers, beef strips, iodine, matches, wire, "sunglasses" (night-vision glasses, in fact), a plastic bottle, and a serrated knife. By the end of the chapter, she has already used the knife, the wire, and the sleeping bag, and her conclusion that it was the right thing to do seems valid.
3. Answers will vary. Katniss shows a lack of sympathy and impatience with what she considers stupidity.
4. Summaries may include seeing Katniss at the Cornucopia and his participation in the hunting and death of the tribute who lit the fir .

102 *The Hunger Games: A Teaching Guide*

Strategy 15, Reading Dialogue, page 49

1. Katniss says it: it comes at the end of a paragraph in which she speaks, even though there is explanation in between. It cannot be Prim because she answers it, and it is not Mrs. Everdeen because the sentiment doesn't fit her.
2. Clearly one tribute said both the fourth and the eighth quotations: the one who stabbed the tribute and still believes she's dead, despite evidence to the contrary. Nothing else is clear except that consecutive phrases are said by different tributes.
3. They are spoken by the prep team. They are some of the only dialogue with exclamation points, of which there are relatively few, the most notable of which occur when something is life threatening (as when Peeta saves Katniss from Cato by screaming at her to "Run!"). This level of enthusiasm over trivialities is a hallmark of citizens of the Capitol.

Writer's Forum, 3 Writing Dialogue, page 50

1. Answers will vary. Dialogue should show characteristics of Effie Trinket's and Haymitch's speech and be properly punctuated and thoughtfully attributed.

Chapter 12, Finding Water; the Wall of Fire, page 51

1. Katniss says (p. 153) that she cannot remember seeing Peeta after the gong sounded, so it may well be that he was injured covering her escape into the woods rather than fighting at the Cornucopia and that he has no intention of revealing how she got the 11 because he is with the Careers to lead them away from Katniss and keep her safe
2. She plans to assume an expression that makes it appear that she knows what Peeta is doing, to show the sponsors that she can hunt, and to conceal how thirst is affecting her.
3. Students may think it is likely that she would have died of thirst or Haymitch would have had to send her a gift of water.
4. The summary should indicate from Haymitch's view whether Peeta and/or Katniss are achieving what he hoped they would achieve in their first hours in the arena

Chapter 13, On Fire; Treed, page 52

1. In both chapters, Katniss draws attention for her relationship to fire, in one case, safe, synthetic fire, in the other, Gamemaker's deadly, synthetic fire and fireball. The second is more memorable because of the first
2. In Dante's *Inferno*, the poet/narrator loses his way in a dark wood and—guided by the ghost of the Roman poet Virgil—tours hell (the *inferno*) and sees the punishments for various sins. In the seventh pouch of the eighth circle of hell is a *pit of vipers* to torment thieves. This is easy to relate to Haymitch's statement in Chapter 8 (p. 107) that in response to shooting at them the Gamemakers are likely to make Katniss's life "hell in the arena." The *pillar of fire* is a signal of the presence of God in Exodus, though it's not clear what that would mean here. Students may think that like the single pun (p. 78 - see Test: Chapters 1–9, question 3) and the two instances of alliteration with *s* (pp. 158, 315 - see Strategy 23, question 6), there are too few of these literary touches and they are too out of keeping with Katniss's background to work well: they stick out from the overall plain style as not fitting in at all
3. Examples include: p. 164 What is being shown to the audience: "I'm glad for the cameras now."; p. 169 What Haymitch is thinking: "There's only one good reason Haymitch could be withholding water from me."; p. 173 What the Gamemakers are thinking: "It's not hard to follow the Gamemakers' motivation." Students may think it's unrealistic but concede that it's necessary, given the first-person narration
4. Student's flow charts should have consistent symbols to represent various characters and their interactions.

Chapter 14, Tracker Jackers; the Silver Bow; Peeta Saves Katniss, page 53

1. Some students may think Rue was warning Katniss to be careful, while others think she's pointing out a weapon to use on the Career Pack.
2. The Captiol's technological capabilities revealed in the arena, genetic engineering, and (apparently) cosmetic surgery are amazing. It seems clear that the districts only have the minimal technology that will allow them to function in providing whatever goods to the Capitol that are desired. Even the electrified fence to keep them in (in District 12, anyway) is poorly maintained and seldom operational.
3. Answers will vary. Students are likely to agree that Katniss has to turn Glimmer over, that the sheath of arrows does get caught, that Peeta does warn her.
4. Peeta would be aware of the death report, the plan for Glimmer to keep watch, the tracker jacker nest

The Hunger Games: A Teaching Guide 103

falling, running to the lake, returning to find Katniss taking the bow and arrows from Glimmer's body and urging her to run, as Cato comes up behind him.

Strategy 16, Plot—Distinguishing Types of Conflict, page 54

1. The overarching goal for Katniss is to fulfill her promise to Prim and return home from the Hunger Game (pp. 36, 106). As students read further, they will see that Rue is added to this ("'Going to win for both of us now,' I promise." pp. 233–4), and then Peeta.
2. All of these are within the overarching conflicts of Capitol v. Districts and Gamemakers vs. Tributes.

4	Katniss/Peeta v. Haymitch (sober mentoring)	12	Katniss v. environment (find water; evade fire	20	Katniss/Haymitch v. Peeta (attendance at the feast)
5	Being treated as an object v. losing Haymitch's mentoring	13	Katniss v. environment (evade fire treat burns); Katniss v. Career Pack	21	Katniss v. Clove; Katniss v. Thresh
6	Katniss v. Team (Avox)	14	Katniss /Rue v. Career Pack; Katniss v. "nature" (tracker jacker venom); Katniss v. Glimmer (bow and arrows)	22	Katniss's reticence v. Sponsors' desires for romance
7	Katniss v. Gamemakers (attention)	15	Katniss/Rue v. Careers	23	Katniss v. Peeta (noise making hunting impossible; staying within range; missing food)
8	Katniss v. herself over lack of self-control	16	Katniss/Rue v. Careers	24	Katniss/Peeta v. Gamemakers (no water)
9	Prepping for interview v. not revealing past	17	Katniss v. loss of hearing; Katniss v. Careers; Katniss v. Environment (find Rue)	25	Katniss/Peeta v. Mutts; Katniss/Peeta v. Cato; Katniss v. Peeta--> Katniss/Peeta v. Gamemakers/Capitol (1 or 2 victors)
10	Katniss v. Peeta (interview revelation; "superior" attitude)	18	Katniss v. District 1 Boy; Katniss v. the Capitol (w. flowers) Katniss v. Despair	26	Katniss v. Capitol (spin)
11	Katniss v. Peeta/Haymitch (1st move) Katniss v. environment (find water)	19	Katniss v. Environment (find Peeta); Katniss/Peeta v. Environment (find place to hide)	27-	Katniss v. Capitol (spin); Katniss v. Peeta (nature of relationship)

Chapter 15, An Ally and a Plan, page 55

1. In both instances, she became empowered to act within her environment: in the first providing food for her family, in the second, providing food for herself (and Rue and Peeta) in the arena.
2. Answers will vary. Students may wonder what will happen if they end up as the final two tributes alive.
3. They disagree about whether Peeta is really in love with Katniss (Rue) or whether it's an act (Katniss).
4. She is acting rather than reacting for the first time since the very beginning of the Games. She is also making plans that are beyond just staying alive, plans that change the odds of winning.
5. Answers will vary. Because Katniss now has a bow, students may predict that she will use it somehow.
6. Rue knows how long Katniss has been unconscious, so she's been watching her: she therefore knows everything Katniss knows except for her internal, unvoiced thoughts in this chapter.

Writer's Forum 4, Writing First-Person Narration, page 56

1. Students' examples of narration will vary, but should reflect a variety of elements of the first-person POV.

Chapter 16, Blowing Up the Careers' Stash, page 57

1. The Careers have, up till now, not had to spend time or energy seeking food or other supplies. Their reliance on this strategy means that they have not trained to feed themselves, nor used their forays to learn where food is. So they have lost an advantage and had a weakness exposed at the same time.
2. Rue was needed to provide a distraction far from the site from which Katniss attacked the supplies and her intelligence information was critical as well. Katniss's ability as an archer made her able to execute a very quick destruction of a large amount of material.
3. Foxface's actions exposed the fact that the area around the pyramid had been mined, which formed a crucial part of Katniss's final plan
4. Students' timelines should reflect the important occurrences in the chapter.

Chapter 17, Katniss Loses Her Hearing; Rue in Trouble, page 58

1. As a hunter and a tribute, Katniss relies on her hearing to alert her to both food and danger.

2. It seems to have succeeded in leaving the Careers at a deficit and also impacting Cato's stability.
3. They believe that the person who blew up their supplies is dead.
4. She is very careful, very thorough, and patient. The Careers, in contrast, are impatient, not thorough, and careless.
5. The dictionary meanings suggest random mingling or things scattered together, while Collins uses it to mean a careful interweaving, done by design and with precision.
6. Answers will vary. Possible response: the spear was already thrown before Katniss broke into the clearing and/or the attacker misjudged how far away she was. Alternatively, students may think that the move is indefensible and fault Collins, a view that's supported by the change to the scene in the movie.
7. Students' graphs should be reasonable depictions of Katniss's emotional highs and lows in this chapter.

Strategy 17, Engaging with Text Through Imaging, page 59

1. Multiple chapters: knowing when it's dawn from the birdsong; knowing when the hovercraft is coming from the birdsong; knowing how many have died from the cannon shots. Chapter 11: hearing (and avoiding) the blade thrown by the District 2 girl; being alerted to the starting of the fire and the Career ack; recognizing Peeta's voice. Chapter 13: hearing and evading fireballs hearing the Careers coming. Chapter 14: understanding that Peeta wants her to run away. Chapter 15: hearing the twig snap the signals Rue's presence. Chapter 16: learning the mockingjay signal; overhearing Careers' conversation. Chapter 17: hearing laugh that alerts her to Foxface's presence; hearing Rue's cries for help.
2. Answers will vary. Possible responses: Touch: p. 3 bed is "cold"; p. 31 "burning" bread; p. 170 "slippery earth"; p. 176 hairs "crumble." Taste: p. 31 "hearty" bread; p. 55 "sweet, creamy" hot chocolate; p. 201 "sharp, sweet taste" of parsnip; p. 202 "delicious meat that's so fatty."
3. Answers will vary. Drawings or writings about images should reflect a scene from ea h chapter.

Strategy 18, Understanding Cliffhangers, page 60

1. Cliffhangers: Ch. 1 - the choosing of Prim as tribute; Ch. 3 - discovering how important Haymitch is to her future; Ch. 4 - concluding that Peeta is planning to kill her; Ch. 7 - shooting the apple and walking out of the Gamemakers' session without being dismissed; Ch. 8 - learning that Peeta wants to be coached alone; Ch. 9 - hearing Peeta's interview revelation; Ch. 11 - learning that Peeta has joined the Career pack; Ch. 12 - seeing the wall of fire descending Ch. 13 - seeing Rue point to something above Katniss's head; Ch. 14 - believing that she's being devoured by ants, Katniss blacks out; Ch. 15 - having the idea for a(n unrevealed) plan; Ch. 16 - being blown back by the blast that targets the Careers' supplies; Ch. 17 - seeing Rue stabbed; Ch. 18 - hearing the rule change and crying out; Ch. 20 - succeeding in getting Peeta to sleep so she can attend the feast; Ch. 21 - blacking out; Ch. 24 running to try to escape what's chasing Cato; Ch. 26 - realizing that the most dangerous part of the Hunger Games is starting; Ch. 27 - returning to District 12, uncertain about Gale, Peeta, and whether President Snow is satisfied with her performanc .

Other types of chapter endings: Ch. 2 - rounding off the reaping; Ch. 5 - thinking she's made the perfect strategic response to Peeta's compliment; Ch. 6 imagining the Avox feeling she's been avenged when Katniss dies in the Games; Ch. 10 - hearing the announcement of the Games beginning; Ch. 19 - announcing Peeta's gift of broth; Ch. 22 - confirming that romance gets gifts when H ymitch sends a feast; Ch. 23 - realizing that Peeta's berries killed Foxface; Ch. 25 - hearing the announcement of two victors.

Chapter 18, Rue's Death; Rule Change, page 61

1. Katniss protects, loves, trusts, and teases both of them. Initially, Katniss is all that stands between Prim and starvation, but over time, the actions of Katniss, Prim, Gale, and Mrs. Everdeen have changed that, so that Prim now has a support network. Rue, in the arena, is alone except for Katniss.
2. Some students may say that because Prim and Rue are similar (age, size, mien), and because Katniss has a similar relationship to them, they have become melded in her mind. Others may feel that this rings false.
3. The fact that this is the first gift given by a District to a tribute that asn't theirs could be highly significant Katniss has created all kinds of bonds within her district, mostly driven by the need to feed her family, but now she is forging links outside her district—one of the key things that the Games are designed to prevent.
4. Katniss wants to talk to Peeta because after Rue's death, she understands what he meant on the roof about wanting to die as himself. Some students may question this whole thread because Katniss's objection to the interview preparation was that she didn't want to be a trained dog, so it's unclear why she didn't understand what Peeta meant as soon as he said it in Chapter 10.

The Hunger Games: A Teaching Guide 105

5.

Choice	Type	Motivation	Information	Extent
Katniss kills the District 1 tribute or lets him live	Terrorized choice (due to both the Capitol and the fact that he killed Rue)	Seeking a theoretical good (vengeance); Seeking life for herself	Partial info (she doesn't wait to see what he does next; true as far as it goes; full awareness	Final choice

Strategy 19, Analyzing Lyrics, pages 62–63

1. The lullaby Katniss sings is an offer of safety and comfort in simple, natural surroundings. The elements that make up the scene—a grassy meadow, a willow tree, daisies, leaves, and moonbeams—are all beautiful and benign. The words invite the hearer to sleep safely in a world in which troubles can be set aside and dreams will come true. It has two verses and a chorus, each being a quatrain. Every line has end rhyme, which can be either perfect rhyme or consonance, the chorus has initial identical rhyme of every line, and there is occasional internal rhyme, close rhyme, and interlaced rhyme. Students may point out the awkwardness of "let your troubles lay"—some may find it acceptable to make the rhyme others may not.
2. The tender, loving song creates a break in the terrifying sequence of compulsory murders.
3. Answers will vary depending on the lullaby chosen.

Writer's Forum 5, Writing Lyrics, page 64

1. Answers will vary. The words of the anthem should be appropriate to the Capitol of Panem.

Test, Chapters 10–18, page 65

Vocabulary
1. These words are related to the preparation of the tributes for the arena.
2. These words are related to Katniss's choice to ignore Haymitch's advice and what she acquired as a result.
3. These words are related to Katniss's experience with the wall of fire and the fireball.
4. These words are related to Rue pointing out the tracker jacker nest to Katniss and Katniss sawing the branch to drop it on the Career pack below.
5. These words describe Glimmer when Katniss went back to claim the silver bow.
6. These words are related to the successful attempt to blow up the Career's supplies.

Essay Topics
1. No, Haymitch does not stick to the deal, since he continues to support both tributes, each of whom disobeyed him. Answers about why may vary. Haymitch may have seen that their choices had value and did not diminish their chances, so he stuck with them.
2. Students may cite Katniss waiting for the iodine to work before drinking the water; refraining from breaking into the crackers and dried beef too soon; continuing to search for water when she barely could; making sure to cook the rabbit rather than risk rabbit fever; taking time to analyze the berries when she was seeking water; and backing off and biding her time when she wanted to go to the feast and Peeta didn't want her to.
3. Answers will vary, depending on the show chosen. Students should choose appropriate categories.
4. District 1 - luxury items (pp. 69, 74); District 3 - factories: televisions, automobiles, explosives (pp. 66, 219); District 4 - fishing (p. 66, 97); District 11 - agriculture: orchards (pp. 66, 97-98, 200); District 12 - coal (p. 4); District 13 - graphite mining (p. 74). Maps will vary, depending on students' knowledge of geography and how they apply the information from Chapter 1.
5. See answer to Chapter 11, question 2. Additional items: burn medicine - ability to acquire leaves for stings and edible berries that Rue identified New items: waterskin, nuts and roots, a bit of rabbit, extra socks, a slingshot, several knifes, two spearheads, a flashlight a pouch, a first-aid kit (on . 257, this is found to hold bandages, fever-reduction pills, and medicine to soothe an upset stomach) a bottle of water, dried fruit. Students' predictions will vary. They may expect that the first-aid kit will be used to treat eeta.
6. Some students may think that Rue's attraction to the mockingjay pin is personal, so not terribly significant. Others may think any reference to mockingjays or interaction with mockingjays smacks of rebellion.
7. Answers will vary. Some students may say that Haymitch is sarcastic: Katniss is not often sweet. Others may say that sarcastic use of an endearment is as close as Haymitch can get to showing affection after all that he's been through (but when they read Chapter 26 and Haymitch kisses her forehead after calling her *sweetheart*, they may conclude that his tone has changed). Peeta first uses it on the roof when he's told Katniss something deeply personal and she hasn't understood: he seems to be mimicking Haymitch. (He may be referencing Haymitch again when he answers her from the mudbank, in Chapter 19, but it may

also be a shorthand for her to identify him by, since he is the only one in the arena who would call her that. Students may suspect that he does it ironically so that he can do it at all - he doesn't expect to ever be able to speak to her in true endearments that are given and taken at face value.
8. The being who is a girl to the other tributes is in the next moment a predator to them. They lose their humanity in the context of the arena and become predators and prey.
9. Maps will vary based on the medium used and how well the students are able to interpret the description in the book and convey it in a 2-D or 3-D form.
10. Katniss impressed the Gamemakers by shooting an apple out of the mouth of their roasted pig. She blows up the careers' supplies by shooting open a bag of apples so that they fell on the mines, which exploded.

PART III THE VICTOR—Chapter 19, Finding Wounded Peeta; the Cave, page 66

1. If Katniss doesn't seek out Peeta, she'll be a pariah upon returning to District 12, and will lose all hope of receiving any more gifts from sponsors. Students may mention that she makes no reference to friendship or owing him for the bread at this juncture.
2. Answers will vary. Besides trying to keep Katniss from running to the Cornucopia and fighting Cato to allow her to escape, he may have deflected atta ks from her at the launch site, led the Careers away from where he knew she was, lied about her habits and talents to encourage them to search in unlikely places, etc.
3. Katniss reasons that Peeta must be near water (although it's never made clear how he avoided getting sick from untreated water). She reasons that the stream is a better shot than the pools because one could move to different spots along it. Her first physical lue is a bloody smear that appears to have been wiped in an effort to erase it. His voice answering her finally helps her locate him
4. Because of Peeta's injured leg (where Cato cut him), they only manage to get 50 yards downstream and 20 yards away from the stream into a sort of cave structure.
5. She has concluded that he is "great" at acting like he's in love (i.e., faking it). She still assumes that he is faking.
6. She applies prior knowledge in considering which of the remaining tributes pose the greatest threat; in determining where to go to seek Peeta; in treating Peeta's burn, stings, and deep cut; in creating a blind for the cave; in trying to figure out how to beh ve like she's in love.

Writer's Forum 6, Writing Description, page 67

1. Sound and sight.
2. Answers will vary. Depending on the phenomenon they choose and the techniques they use to describe it.

Chapter 20, Prim's Goat; Invitation to a Feast, page 68

1. The fact that when Katniss and Peeta kiss and speak romantically, they receive gifts.
2. Katniss lies about the Avox (p. 82–3), and while Peeta doesn't confront her about it, he is very solicitous immediately after and may have known. He also doesn't comment on her response when he asks about how serious his wound is (p. 256), but again, while he doesn't challenge the answer, he's a smart guy, and he may know she's lying. The fact that he "looks almost sorry for [Katniss]" shortly after may signal that he not only knows how bad it is, but also that she's not really able to properly treat it. She also lies when she says he's cooler (p. 273), but the trumpets sound, so Peeta doesn't respond. Then she lies about her intentions with regard to the feast. When he identifies her as a lia , he mentioned her comment about the goat (which students may not class as a lie, but more something Katniss said to avoid getting personal), saying he was cooler, and her comment about the feast, so he seems to be able to read her (and, students may note, enormously better than she can read him). He's onto her lie about the "sugar berries," too, but physical force and the effects of the syrup overpower him. Katniss's triumph is somewhat hollow.
3. Answers will vary. Students may think that he hopes to draw away tributes who might attack her.
4. She says she is going to the feast because if she didn't the audience would hate her and she would hate herself.
5. Students should include the essential facts of both what really happened and the story Katniss tells to avoid getting District 12 people in trouble.

Writer's Forum 7, Composing an Anecdote, page 69

1. Answers will vary. Students may have Katniss play up her doubts of the usefulness of Peeta's skill and her surprise when she sees how well he did and realizes that—with the Careers tramping around looking for him and his being unable to move—it really did save him.

The Hunger Games: A Teaching Guide 107

Chapter 21, The Gamemaker's Feast; Death and Medicine, page 70

1. It made her able to destroy the Careers' supplies; it enabled her to learn Foxface's *modus operandi*; it gave her knowledge of the leaves to relieve stings and another type of edible berry; it allowed her to get more insight into Cato; it earned her a gift of bread; in Rue's death, it gave her a deeper understanding of what Peeta meant on the roof; it got her important supplies, including the first-aid kit from the District 1 boy and Rue's socks.
2. Clove calls Katniss "District Twelve" minimizing her humanity. Thresh calls her "Fire Girl," acknowledging what Cinna sees as her essence (being spirited).
3. Either she didn't want to slow down her running to apply them or Collins forgot Katniss had them.
4. Answers will vary. Students may object to this as an unlikely mix of the lullaby to Prim and Rue's death
5. Thresh saw Clove's attack, interacted with Katniss and ran off with both remaining backpacks.

Chapter 22, Feelings on Display; Haymitch's Feast, page 71

1. Answers may vary. Students may point out that there's already been a lot of evidence that Peeta has been telling the truth all along. In addition, what he says about Mr. Everdeen singing echoes what Katniss said earlier, and Katniss not only confirms that she sang the first y of school and that there was a red plaid dress in the family but also that the story has "the ring of truth" (p. 301) to the point that Katniss wonders if she's been wrong about Peeta being strategic from the beginning.
2. It helps to explain why he would have come to see Katniss in the Justice Building and given her cookies.
3. Having lived in town and had little opportunity to learn about nature and "wild" places, he views them with fear.
4. Katniss receives burn medicine after she prepares to drop the tracker jacker the following morning (p. 188); bread after she avenges Rue's death, sings to her, and covers her in flowers (. 238); broth after she kisses Peeta (p. 261); sleeping syrup after she reaches a stalemate with Peeta in getting medicine to save his life (p. 276); a feast after saying that Peeta doesn't have much competition anywhere (p. 302).

Chapter 23, Thresh's Death; Foxface's Death, page 72

1. This is the second time that Katniss has used the word in the book (the first as in reference to the child in District 11 whom the Peacekeepers killed for taking a pair of the night-vision glasses). It shows a change in her perception of what is going on in the arena
2. Katniss sees the "full moon" in the arena on her 22nd day away from home and had seen the full moon at home shortly before she left. This is indeterminate: the moon may or may not be real, but it could be.
3. Katniss's focus since she was 11 has been on feeding her family: she has spent her time in pursuit of food, learned skills to help her acquire and trade food, and practiced techniques to secure various kinds of food. If she is a victor, all of this will no longer be necessary, leaving a huge gap in her life.
4. She knows how Foxface operates, avoiding confrontations and stealing little bits so as not to be suspected.
5. Students should look for mentions of the words *dawn*, *birdsong*, *light* to help them identify the start of each new day.

Strategy 20, Revising Hypotheses, page 73

1. It's not really clear that Katniss's ability to judge others has improved—though perhaps the sign that she even thought that Peeta's story about when he fell in love with her had the ring of truth may be hopeful.
2. Answers will vary depending on students' initial hypotheses and whether the book has provided any evidence thus far that has a bearing on it.

Chapter 24, Last Night in the Cave; Driven to the Lake, page 74

1. Students may recall Peeta's fear of nature and think it's logical that he wouldn't be able to differentiate berries. On the other hand, Peeta is an artist, and Katniss remarked on his ability to capture light and shadow in his camouflage with limited hance for observation (p.96), and skillful observation of nature saved his life (p. 252). Without further explanation, it may seem unlikely to students that he would mistake them. Students who have read *Catching Fire*, where Peeta's powers of observation are highlighted further, may provide additional evidence. The handling in the movie eliminates this apparent conflict
2. There really hasn't been any evidence to support that Foxface would have recognized a trick and was only seduced into eating the berries by Peeta's genuine intention to eat them.
3. Possible response: A final fight in the open means nothing will obscure the audienc s view of any part of it.
4. When she is seeking Peeta, she wants to avoid mockingjays so she can call him very softly without the birds repeating her calls. In this chapter, she simply enjoys their music, listening to how it develops.

5. In her desperate fear, Katniss has forgotten Peeta and his wounded leg.
6. Since he is with Katniss for the whole chapter, he will know everything except her interior thoughts.

Writer's Forum 8, Writing a Possible Ending, page 75

1. Answers will vary. Students' ending should be consistent with the story development through Chapter 24.

Chapter 25, Muttations; Second Rule Change; More Berries; Victors, page 76

1. Students should note that mutts' ability to stand on their hind legs, move their wrists, their 4-inch razor-sharp claws, thick fur of varying colors (to match tributes' hair), their ability to communicate with high-pitched yipping, that their eyes are identifiable as the tribute , matching their jewel-inlaid collar numbers
2. Katniss kills Cato out of pity.
3. **Situation 1**: Stalemate with Peeta over feast attendance. Apparent Choice: Katniss doesn't go or Peeta will go with her. Choice made: Katniss (with Haymitch's help) makes sure Peeta is asleep so he can't go. Result: Katniss goes and saves Peeta's life, receiving a non-life-threatening injury. **Situation 2**: Stalemate with Cato who has Peeta in a headlock. Apparent Choice: If Katniss shoots Cato to kill him, he will pull Peeta off the Cornucopia with him when he dies and the mutts will get Peeta; if she doesn't, he will kill break Peeta's neck. Choice made: At Peeta's suggestion, Katniss shoots Cato's hand. Result: Cato releases Peeta and falls off the Cornucopia; Katniss grabs Peeta and keeps him on top. **Situation 3**: Stalemate with Peeta after rule change over who will die. Apparent Choice: Either Peeta or Katniss has to die. Choice: They both prepare to commit suicide. Result: The rules are changed to allow them both to live.
4. Answers may vary. Students may mention the status of Katniss's and Peeta's relationship and whether there will be repercussions for having not bent to the rule change as two key elements needing tying up.

Chapter 26, Recovery Period; Haymitch's Warning, page 77

1. Recalling the time when she called one of the tributes *girl* and then *predator*, Katniss now uses a word that she and Peeta both formerly used of sick animals outside the bounds of District 12 to describe herself, suggesting the negative effects that the experience of the Hunger Games has had on her.
2. It is a statement meant to be open to two interpretations: that he is already so much in love or that he knows very well how to act strategically. The first interpretation is correct
3. The five motivations are taking part in the game , anger at the Capitol, concern about District 12's response, acting out of common decency, and caring for Peeta.
4. The new dangers are revealed through Cinna's costume design and careful comment, as well as through Haymitch's more direct warning.

Strategy 21, Interpreting Irony, page 78

1. **Verbal Irony**: "I'm sure the arena will be full of bags of flour for me to huck at people" (Peeta, p. 90). **Dramatic Irony**: That the reader understands Peeta's motivation better than Katniss. That the reader knows that Katniss has found water before she does (p. 170). **Situational Irony**: That Peeta comes to wish that Haymitch had a drink, when it had seemed impossible to stop him from drinking (p. 99). That the Capitol's rule that volunteers can replace chosen tributes allows Katniss, who won, to replace Prim, who didn't have the skills or knowledge to have a chance. That the Capitol's starving of District 12 provoked the situation in which Katniss learned the skills she used in the arena. That Katniss used the berries that the Gamemakers put in the arena to kill unwary tributes to put the Gamemakers themselves in a bind.
2. It may be considered ironic that the story has become part of the entertainment industry that it critiques. It is not ironic that people choose to watch it because they are watching acting, not reality.

Strategy 22, Tracing the Hero's Journey, page 79

1. Possible responses: I - Katniss is **Called** indirectly when Prim's name is chosen. II - Although Katniss accepts the **Call** initially, her refusal to cooperate with Haymitch in preparing for the interview is a **Refusal**, since she will likely need sponsors to have any chance of winning. III - Cinna is a protector (similar, in ways, to Cinderella's fairy godmother who supplied her with a dress to go to the ball) and the assistance from sponsors outside the arena that float down on silver para hutes functions as **Supernatural Aid.** IV - The launch pad into the arena is the **First Threshold**, and V - the arena is the **Belly of the Whale** by which Katniss is swallowed (also the cave) . VI - the time in the arena is the **Road of Trials**. VII/VIII- the **Magic Flight** is accomplished by hovercraft (though her protector is not with her), and that and her time in the hospital are her **Crossing of the Return Threshold**. To come: IX - Her status as victor will trans-

The Hunger Games: A Teaching Guide 109

fer over to the first world where she will live in the Victor's Village when she returns home, making her **Master of Two Worlds**. X - It remains to be seen whether she achieves **Freedom to Live**.

Strategy 23, Analyzing Diction and Style, page 80

1. Haymitch or Peeta.
2. Katniss uses sentence fragments to mirror actual conversation and thought, which are not always in full sentences ("At home. The iced ones, for the bakery," p. 96). This shows disjointed thought processes ("Good for bee stings, too. Mud. Mud. Mud!" (p. 170); halting consideration ("He's not particularly handsome. Not in the way that causes sponsors to rain gifts on you" p. 306); and the addition of tag sentiments ("My mother was very beautiful once, too. Or so they tell me." p. 3).
3. Clove ("We're going to kill you. Just like we did your pathetic little ally . . . then I think we'll just let nature take care of Lover Boy. . . . "I think we'll start with your mouth." p. 285; "Let's get started." p. 286).
4. Caesar Flickerman
5. Answers will vary. Students may suggest that this feature requires readers to attend closely to context and not make assumptions about Collins's word use.
6. With only two uses, it doesn't really become an integrated aspect of her style, and since she is not literary, it doesn't make sense and stands out as unlikely.

Chapter 27, Highlights; Exit Interview; Train Ride Home, pages 81–82

1. It seems as if the filmmakers might have been looking for this ending from the beginning and maybe supporting these particular tributes. Their choice of ending seems like confirmation This could either be to support Katniss and Peeta or to make it appear that the Capitol planned this ending all along.
2. Students are likely to say that the small man described earlier now clearly seems to wield power and will squelch anything or anyone that might potentially interfere with it.
3. Answers will vary. Possible responses: Haymitch knows that Peeta is now convinced that Katniss is acting out of true affection for him, even if she was pretending to start with, and if they talk, he is astute enough to realize this is not the case. This would make it harder for both of them to be convincing in their public appearances.
4. Since Peeta really is in love, and is also a noble, unselfish person he will do everything he can to cast Katniss in the best possible light - he doesn't need to be told.
5. Her willingness to die with him rather than live without him was probably pretty convincing, without knowing her thoughts about why, as her answer to Caesar's interview question about when she fell for him may have been.
6. It's ironic that while Katniss realized the wildflowers she arranged around Rue might have been "weeds of some sort," (p. 237), she still felt that they were meaningful, but she critiques Peeta's gift of flowers not only because they remind her of Gale but also because they're the tops of wild onions, not flowers as such.
7. She means that she is stopping the show that was done only to survive in the arena.
8. Answers will vary. Possible response: If the Capitol leaves them alone, it is likely they will not be in contact much, due both to Katniss's lack of clarity about her feelings and Gale's presence in District 12.
9. Answers will vary. Possible responses: the entertainment industry, reality television, violence used in "games," the way teen models and actors are portrayed in the press.
10. Answers will vary but summaries should reflect the novel

Strategy 24, Rereading a Book, page 83

1. Students may report a fuller experience of the story, having already learned the vocabulary and sorted out any other misunderstandings. They may also find that they are aware of more patterns and repetitions.

Strategy 25, Identifying Themes, page 84

1. Possible response: Katniss comes to represent district opposition to the Capitol in the arena. When she goes home, she takes the understandings she has gained with her. We don't know the effects this may have.
2. Possible responses: Appearance vs. Reality; Deception vs. Art; Internal vs. External Identity; the Power of Partnerships; Food as Power; Desensitization to and Through Violence; Bread and Circuses.
3. Answers will vary depending on the other "community" book or dystopia chosen for comparison.

Writer's Forum 9, Composing a Book Review, page 85

1. Answers will vary. Reviews must include a summary and evaluation, though they can be intertwined. The evaluation should respond to the main parts of the story and be criteria-based.

Writer's Forum 10, Comparing Two Treatments, page 86

1. Students should address the questions given for guidance. Facts and opinions should be clearly stated and opinions should be supported by evidence. There are too many differences between the book and the movie to list them all here.

   Notable differences include: the point of view is changed to third-person omniscient and material is included that Katniss was not privy to (including scenes with the Gamemakers, Haymitch, and President Snow); the rivalry between Peeta and Gale is not established to the same depth and the love story is downplayed; the relationship between the tributes and Haymitch develops differently, and he communicates with Katniss in the arena via messages in the parachute deliveries, rather than telepathy; Katniss understands Peeta's desire to "die as myself" immediately, giving her less opportunity for personal growth and their relationship less opportunity for growth; the mockingjay pin (which is a gift from Greasy Sae at the Hob before the reaping, rather than Madge, after Katniss has volunteered) is hidden (by Cinna) and noticed by President Snow at the victor's crowning (and only Katniss gets a crown, changing the symbolism); Foxface and Katniss have an early encounter and let each other go; Katniss quickly finds water, focusing the struggles in the arena on encounters with other tributes and the machinations of the Gamemakers, rather than survival; we are shown that Rue's death causes riots in District 11; Katniss does not drug Peeta nor administer medicine to him via a hypodermic needle; Peeta's leg is pretty well healed by the medicine, and the tourniquet and amputation are omitted; Seneca Crane is forced to commit suicide with Nightlock berries. While the novel ends with Katniss dreading having to let go of Peeta's hand, the movie ends with President Snow.

   The most problematic points in the novel are reworked with marked success: the oft-repeated line in the books about shooting at the Gamemakers is given to President Snow, not Katniss—which makes more sense—and only stated once; Katniss cuts Rue out of the net before the spear attack, which is aimed at Katniss and misses her as she stoops to pick up her bow, hitting Rue unintentionally, which also makes more sense; Peeta does not claim to have recognized the Nightlock berries as the ones Katniss had picked, which is more consistent with his character and personality as developed throughout the series.

Test, Chapters 19–27, page 87

Vocabulary

1. *Abate*, *alleviate*, and *quench* refer to lessening as an improvement. *Deplete* and *dwindling* refer to lessening that is undesirable. *Diminishes* can be either positive or negative.
2a. These words name the distinguishing attributes of the tributes besides Katniss who attend the final feast
2b. These words name aspects of Clove's attack on Katniss.
2c. These words describe the sound of the mockingjays as Katniss and Peeta sit by the lake waiting for Cato.

Essay Topics

1. Katniss's sponsors, District 11's sponsors, the supplies she inherited from Rue and took from the District 1 boy, teamwork with Rue and Peeta, Effie's interview coaching, Cinna's costumes, the prep team's work, clues about how to behave from Haymitch, and Peeta's deception of the Careers all contributed to victory.
2. Father: hunting, plants; Mother, Prim: healing; Cinna: her identifying characteristic; Haymitch: how to communicate with someone who isn't present; Rue: healing leaves, another kind of berry, how to interact with Mockingjays; Effie: how to wear a long dress and high heels, how to act in an interview.
3. Music is a way to achieve an intimate connection with nature (mockingjay/humans interaction), of easing pain (Rue's death), of showing unity (Panem anthem). It's "unearthly" beauty (p. 329) makes it the closest thing to the spiritual in the novel.
4. Gale --> Prim (in absentia) for the goat cheese; District 12's salute to Katniss means "thanks"; Katniss --> Mr. Mellark for the cookies; Katniss --> her prep team for their work; Peeta --> Katniss for holding onto him in the chariot; Katniss sarcastically --> the Gamemakers; Katniss --> Cinna for her 1st interview dress; Katniss --> the Gamemakers for saying she can't reveal how she got an 11; Peeta ends his interview with thanks after confessing his love for Katniss; Effie --> Peeta and Katniss for being her best tributes; Peeta mockingly --> Katniss for telling him to stay alive (on the roof); Katniss mockingly and mentally --> Clove for the knife thrown at her; Katniss --> Haymitch for the gift of burn ointment; Katniss --> District 11; Katniss jokingly --> Peeta for reminding her that she can kiss him any time; Peeta --> Katniss for taking care of him and for finding him and for offering him anything he might want; Thresh --> Katniss (her word) by letting her live; Peeta --> Haymitch and Katniss for being well rested; Katniss --> many people at the Victory Banquet; Katniss mentally --> Caesar for the idea that she fell for Peeta when she said his name in the tree. (Katniss's indirect statement p. 90—"But only because someone helped me"— is the closest she comes to thanking Peeta.)

The Hunger Games: A Teaching Guide 111

5. Answers will vary based on the novel chosen for comparison and students' interpretations of the endings.
6. She thought he was going to attack her. It is one of many examples in which Katniss misreads people.
7. Answers will vary. Possible response: With so many people betting on the outcome and so invested in their sponsored tributes, having no victor was not acceptable in terms of public relations.
8. President Snow is upset because the Gamemakers said "one winner" and were forced to make it two or none: it is a crack in their absolute power that can't be allowed.
9. When she: teams up with Rue, ignoring the future and treats her like a sister; decides she doesn't hate the District 1 boy (236); shoots Cato out of pity rather than vengeance; refuses to bend to "one winner."
10. Students may say the title suggests that President Snow / the Capitol is the real victor or Katniss is.
11. Katniss believes that the residents of the Capitol will execute the Gamemakers if there is no victor. They've said there can only be one victor, but if they thought they were going to lose both victors in one blow, they might be forced to accept two victors, rather than none. But it has to be a real possibility—not a fake (same reasoning as with Foxface), and the berries provide that.

THEME PAGES, pages 88–89

Taste
1. Collins posits that tastes—at least the tastes of the Capitol—are indicators of values, and some values and tastes (those that involve children fighting to the death as entertainment and tyranny that le ves a population starving) are worthy of condemnation.
2. Examples of the expression of taste include Rue's and Mr. Everdeen's singing, Peeta's cake decoration, Katniss's choice of gift for Prim, Madge's mockingjay pin. Students may feel that for Katniss, Cinna's costumes are an expression of her taste, and Mrs. Everdeen's and Prim's healing arts are an expression of theirs.

Identity
1. The community creates boundaries for adolescents' choices (laws and rules), provides training and information to help them learn skills and develop talents (education, in school and out), and responds to adolescents' choices with evaluative feedback, both positive and negative.
2. Students may feel that the characters remain essentially who they are.
3. Answers will vary. Students may feel that her status and reputation reflect who she is capable of becoming rather than exactly who she is now.

Integrity
1. Definitions will var . Possible responses: Integrity and honesty amount to the same thing. Integrity is being true to one's idea of virtue. Integrity means doing what's right, no matter what.
2. Answers will vary. Students should support their opinions.
3. If it were true, they would be able to destroy the integrity of the entire citizenry of the districts.
4. People are apt to break laws in order to get enough to eat. Neither the victors in the arena nor the people who are forced to watch the Games can escape the feeling of complicity in the deaths of others.

Courage
1. Answers will vary depending on students' context, understanding, and values.
2. Answers will vary, but are likely to include Peeta's actions to save Katniss.
3. Answers will vary depending on students' interpretation of the various actors' motivations
4. Students are unlikely to think that Collins considers courage guarantees other virtues (Cato is brave).

Friendship and Loyalty
1. Answers will vary depending on students' context, understanding, and values. Katniss and Rue and Katniss and Cinna are most likely to be seen as friends.
2. Students are likely to see Katniss's handling of Rue's death and Peeta's protection of Katniss, despite how she has behaved towards him, as outstanding loyalty.

Leadership and Government
1. Answers will vary depending on students' context, understanding, and values.
2. He leads a corrupt regime that maltreats the citizens of Panem.
3. Students may point out that the entertainment industry supports liberal government in the United States, but they are separate entities. In Panem, the government is the producer of the entertainment (panem et circenses).

Good and Evil
1. Answers will vary depending on students' context, understanding, and values.
2. Katniss overcomes the black and white dichotomy when she says she hates the Capitol, rather than the District 1 boy, and is able to see Cato as a suffering person, not just an enemy.
3. Students' responses will depend in part on their personal values.